BLOOD, BREAD, AND POETRY

Selected Prose 1979–1985

BY ADRIENNE RICH

BLOOD, BREAD, AND POETRY

Selected Prose 1979–1985

Adrienne Rich

W. W. Norton & Company, New York London

Printed in the United States of America.

The text of this book is composed in Avanta, with display type set in Times Roman. Composition and manufacturing by The Haddon Craftsmen, Inc. Book design by B. Klein.

Library of Congress Cataloging-in-Publication Data

Rich, Adrienne.
  Blood, bread, and poetry: Selected prose 1979–1985

  Includes index.
  I. Title.
PS3535.I233B6   1986   811'.54   86–5452

ISBN 0-393-02376-1

W. W. Norton & Company, Inc., 500 Fifth Avenue, New York, N.Y. 10110
W. W. Norton & Company Ltd., 10 Coptic Street, London WC1A 1PU

    4 5 6 7 8 9 0

Contents

Foreword

These essays were not written in an ivory tower. But neither
were they written on the edges of a political organizer's daily
life, or a nine-to-five manual or clerical job, or in prison. My
fifteen or so years in the Women's Liberation movement have
been spent as a writer, a teacher, an editor-publisher, a pam-
phleteer, a lecturer, and a sometimes activist. Before and
throughout, I have been a poet.

I had been looking for the Women's Liberation movement
since the 1950s. I came into it in 1970. A National Women's
Strike for Equality was called on August 26 of that year, and
thousands of women marched in New York City, 2,000 in San
Francisco, 5,000 in Boston. I was in rural Vermont at the time.
A friend shipped up to me a bundle of pamphlets from the
New York movement, and so I went out to distribute Marge
Piercy's "The Grand Coulee Damn" and Pat Mainardi's "The
Politics of Housework" in small public libraries and clinics and
bookstores. Even at the time, I wondered a bit about their
impact then and there, aimed as they were at young urban
political women; yet it was an action of a kind, a statement to
myself, that I wanted and needed what this movement was
affirming: the solidarity and empowering of women.

For most of my life, I had heard the word *feminist* spoken
in pejoration and derision. The phrase *women's liberation*
was illuminating to me, and *feminism* was beginning to res-
onate with fresh and positive meaning. I identified myself as
a radical feminist, and soon after—not as a political act
but out of powerful and unmistakable feelings—as a les-
bian.[1]

In the late 1960s radical feminism defined itself as "an
independent revolutionary movement of women," an "autono-
mous women's movement." This meant that women already
active in movements for social justice were refusing to post-
pone issues of gender injustice, male chauvinism, and sexual
politics till "after the revolution." Women were moving from
organizing women for the male Left into setting their own
priorities, creating their own organizations. As one group, The
Feminists (New York) stated, "Class separation between men
and women is a political division. . . . All political classes grew
out of the male-and-female role system, were modeled on it,
and are rationalized by it and its premises." In the words of the
Redstockings Manifesto: "We identify with all women. We
define our best interest as that of the poorest, most brutally
exploited women."[2]

The naming as political of women's personal experiences, to
be explored and compared in consciousness-raising sessions,
was a keystone of radical-feminist theory. The consciousness-
raising session itself, with its emphasis on each woman's indi-
vidual testimony, which was then to be "related and general-

1. At no time have I ever defined myself as, or considered myself, a lesbian separatist.
I have worked with self-defined separatists and have recognized the importance of
separatism as grounding and strategy. I have opposed it as a pressure to conformity
and where it seemed to derive from biological determinism. The necessity for autono-
mous women's groups still seems obvious to me.

2. *Women's Liberation—Notes from the Second Year: Major Writings of the Radi-
cal Feminists,* ed. Shulamith Firestone and Anne Koedt (New York, 1970), pp.
113–114.

ized" as a grounding for theory and organizing, was central to radical-feminist practice.[3]

Rereading some of the early documents, you can feel the wrench and strain of this movement, born in the Civil Rights movement and the Left (many of its initiators literally daughters of the Old Left), trying to separate itself from Leftist sexism and dogmatism, shape a feminist theory based on female experience, and remain connected to a radical imagining of social transformation. This was radical feminism as I encountered it in New York in 1969: in acute rebellion against a politics in which theory, priorities, leadership were a male preserve; thousands of women streaming into a women's movement which the Left first trivialized, then denounced and tried to subvert.

At the same time, Black women were looking critically both at the Black Liberation movement (male in image and rhetoric) and the Women's Liberation movement (white in image and unexamined assumptions). Black women's organizing as women under the conditions of racism was at that point invisible to the mainstream media and to many white feminists. But it was an ongoing fact of Black community history.[4]

3. Kathie Sarachild, "A Program for Feminist 'Consciousness-Raising,' " in *Women's Liberation—Notes from the Second Year,* pp. 78–80.

4. By 1970, in her preface to an anthology called *The Black Woman* (New York: Signet), Toni Cade (Bambara) could write:

> Throughout the country in recent years, Black women have been forming work-study groups, discussion clubs, cooperative nurseries, cooperative businesses, consumer education groups, women's workshops on the campuses, women's caucuses within existing organizations, Afro-American women's magazines. From time to time they have organized seminars on the Role of the Black Woman, conferences on the Crisis Facing the Black Woman, have provided tapes on the Attitude of European Men Toward Black Women, working papers on the Position of the Black Woman in America; they have begun correspondence with sisters in Vietnam, Guatemala, Algeria, Ghana. . . . formed alliances on a Third World Women plank. They are women who have not, it would seem, been duped by the prevailing notions of "woman" but who have maintained a critical stance.

Bernice Reagon notes that "a majority of the people who were in jail [in the Civil

With a three hundred fifty years' struggle for Black libera-
tion both behind them and continuing, Black women began to
address the emerging new white women's movement as well as
each other and other sisters of color. The radical-feminist claim
to identify with all women was to undergo severe challenge. To
believe that it was right to identify with all women, to wish
deeply and sincerely to do so, was not enough. (I still hear the
voice of a Black feminist saying with passionate factuality: *But
you don't know us!*) White feminism had on its hands, cer-
tainly, a voluminous task of redefining and re-examining white
patriarchy, the dominant Western male culture whose institu-
tions and ideologies have spread across the world. But white
women are situated within white patriarchy as well as against
it. And many of us were then and have been since thinking and
speaking unconsciously from within as well as in conscious
opposition.

In *On Lies, Secrets, and Silence* (1979), I wrote of the loss
and obscuring of the history and culture women need in shap-
ing a future; of the power of women's community (which was
throughout the seventies and is still in the eighties creating
new institutions and making demands of existing ones); of
ethical and creative possibilities called forth by a new lesbian-
feminist consciousness. That book, like this one, came out of
a movement, which in turn generated a cultural climate. Rape-
crisis hotlines, battered-women's shelters, houses for women
emerging from psychiatric abuse, feminist health and abortion
clinics, grass-roots feminist publications, the work of dedicated
activists fueled my understanding, my images, and my words.

Rights movement] were women. . . . When you look and see who comes to the mass
meetings / It is Black women who are there every night" (Bernice Johnson Reagon,
"My Black Mothers and Sisters or On Beginning a Cultural Autobiography," *Feminist
Studies* 8, no. 1 [Spring 1981]: 95). See also Paula Giddings, *When and Where I Enter:
The Impact of Black Women on Race and Sex in America* (New York: Morrow, 1984).

I wrote and signed my words as an individual, but they were part of a collective ferment.

Every writer is touched by "influences," seeks the validation of a community (if only of the listening dead), is connected somewhere. But the relation between individual writer and political movement is often predicated as mysterious and problematic. Is the writer a privileged figure who somehow gets the power of definition, of describing the movement to itself? Does the movement inevitably seek to regulate and censor the writer's imagination? Does the writer secretly tame her imagination in order to defend her cause? But how, then, is it "her" cause? Where does the imagination get its images anyway?

Trying to construct ideas and images afresh, by staying close to concrete experience, for the purpose of alleviating a common reality that is felt to be intolerable—this seems to me fair work for the imagination. Even a hang-glider has to work with the wind or come crashing down on the cliffs. There is a rarely described dynamic between the writer who is part of a radical movement and the movement which is constantly creating itself through many kinds of testimony, actions, new experiences to which the writer, within her individual limits, is witness and in some of which she is participant.[5] (What writing and politics have most in common, perhaps, is that both are creative processes requiring many false starts and strange go-rounds, many hard choices.)

The essays in this book are to some extent a time line of my travels since 1978. I have revised in order to tighten, to clarify what had seemed confusing in earlier versions, and in response to some criticisms. I have updated certain footnotes to make

5. Some descriptions of this dynamic can be found in Margaret Randall's *Risking a Somersault in the Air: Conversations with Nicaraguan Writers* (San Francisco: Solidarity Publications, 1984).

the book more currently useful. But the essays are indicative of a continuing exploration, not of a destination. The white radical feminist is confronted by the analysis by women of color of simultaneity of oppressions. For women in whose experience —and in whose theory, therefore—sex, race, and class converge as points of exploitation, there is no "primary oppression" or "contradiction," and it is not patriarchy alone that must be comprehended and dismantled. I began to understand that this was as true—in a different way—for white and middle-class women, that patriarchy has no pure and simple existence in this world any more than class does. In the final essay of *On Lies, Secrets, and Silence,* I had tried to grapple with racism and racial identity, but still with a primarily anti-patriarchal grappling hook. My question there was, How does racism hinder and defeat the lesbian-feminist, or radical-feminist, vision of woman identification; how much is it a residue of loyalties to white men? But the woman trying to fit racism and class into a strictly radical-feminist analysis finds that the box won't pack. The woman who seeks the experiential grounding of identity politics realizes that as Jew, white, woman, lesbian, middle-class, she herself has a complex identity. Further, that her very citizenship, which gives her both grief and privilege, is part of her identity: her U.S. passport, in this world, is part of her body, and she lives under a very specific patriarchy.

The roots of this further exploration are events and impressions, public and personal, large and small. The election of Reagan; a swiftly widening gulf between rich and poor in the United States; the proliferation of nuclear missiles world-wide; a growing brazenness of racist and anti-Semitic hatred and violence; an increasingly visible and vocal international movement of women of color; the richly difficult contradictions of emerging Jewish feminism. Discontent with the polarizing impulses within radical feminism, with the academization of Women's Studies, with how easily, in a society turning Rightward, feminism can blur into female enclave, how feminist affirmation of women can slide into mere idealism. An urgent sense of the 1980s as offering new opportunities in exchange for more complicated commitments. I co-edited a lesbian-feminist quarterly, worked with a Jewish-lesbian study group, found myself teaching a new generation of youth, a generation labeled "apolitical" (as my own had been) and "postfeminist." Like many other North Americans in this decade, I studied with the Sandinistas in Nicaragua—lessons of the heart as well as the head. Through periodicals, correspondence, conferences, I was also learning about feminist movements in India, the Caribbean, Latin America, the Pacific; studying the political geography of the Middle East and the terrain of North American Jewish experience. The history of African women's specific sufferings under, and resistance to, apartheid became visible to me through the work of Joyce Sikakane, Ellen Kuzwayo, Hilda Bernstein, Joyce Goodwin, and through SISA (Sisterhood in Support of Sisters in South Africa, an organization of women of color in the United States providing material support for Black South African women). New questions were emerging from a newly visible range of female experience. In and out of all this: conversations, arguments, withdrawals; times of feeling tired, angry, stuck, blocked; picking up new fire from others close at hand, and from strangers. Poetry continuously there: a kind of knowledge.

It's possible that for some readers there is too little about poetry in these pages. I first began writing prose *about* poetry —reviews, critical essays, forewords to other poets' books. More recently, I have written less about poems themselves and more about the social and historical conditions of their making. The title essay attempts to link the two. More and more, my question about poetry has been one I ask in that essay: *What happens to the heart of the artist, here in North America?*

Santa Cruz, California   Adrienne Rich
February 1986

Acknowledgments

Most of the writings in this book exist because I was asked for a review, a lecture, an article, a keynote address. I thank those who gave me the occasion to work out ideas on paper and the forum to present them. I thank the many friends who criticized early and late drafts. My individual hand and heart are responsible for the gaps in perception or interpretation.

I am grateful to three women on two coasts who typed or retyped most of this book with intelligence, skill, and understanding: Edna McGlynn, Kirsten Allrud, Birdie Flynn. Once more, I thank Carol Flechner for her high standards as manuscript editor.

For ten years' companionship, challenge, and support, I am joyfully indebted to Michelle Cliff.

BLOOD, BREAD, AND POETRY

Selected Prose 1979–1985

What Does a Woman Need to Know? (1979)

I have been very much moved that you, the class of 1979, chose me for your commencement speaker. It is important to me to be here, in part because Smith is one of the original colleges for women, but also because she has chosen to continue identifying herself as a women's college. We are at a point in history where this fact has enormous potential, even if that potential is as yet unrealized. The possibilities for the future education of women that haunt these buildings and grounds are enormous, when we think of what an independent women's college might be: a college dedicated both to teaching women what women need to know and, by the same token, to changing the landscape of knowledge itself. The germ of those possibilities lies symbolically in The Sophia Smith Collection, an archive much in need of expansion and increase, but which by its very existence makes the statement that women's lives and work are valued here and that our foresisters, buried and diminished in male-centered scholarship, are a living presence, necessary and precious to us.

Suppose we were to ask ourselves simply: What does a

Commencement address, Smith College, Northampton, Massachusetts, 1979.

woman need to know to become a self-conscious, self-defining human being? Doesn't she need a knowledge of her own history, of her much-politicized female body, of the creative genius of women of the past—the skills and crafts and techniques and visions possessed by women in other times and cultures, and how they have been rendered anonymous, censored, interrupted, devalued? Doesn't she, as one of that majority who are still denied equal rights as citizens, enslaved as sexual prey, unpaid or underpaid as workers, withheld from her own power —doesn't she need an analysis of her condition, a knowledge of the women thinkers of the past who have reflected on it, a knowledge, too, of women's world-wide individual rebellions and organized movements against economic and social injustice, and how these have been fragmented and silenced?

Doesn't she need to know how seemingly natural states of being, like heterosexuality, like motherhood, have been enforced and institutionalized to deprive her of power? Without such education, women have lived and continue to live in ignorance of our collective context, vulnerable to the projections of men's fantasies about us as they appear in art, in literature, in the sciences, in the media, in the so-called humanistic studies. I suggest that not anatomy, but enforced ignorance, has been a crucial key to our powerlessness.

There is—and I say this with sorrow—there is no women's college today which is providing young women with the education they need for survival as whole persons in a world which denies women wholeness—that knowledge which, in the words of Coleridge, "returns again as power." The existence of Women's Studies courses offers at least some kind of life line. But even Women's Studies can amount simply to compensatory history; too often they fail to challenge the intellectual and political structures that must be challenged if women as a group are ever to come into collective, nonexclusionary freedom. The belief that established science and scholarship—which have so relentlessly excluded women from their making —are "objective" and "value-free" and that feminist studies are "unscholarly," "biased," and "ideological" dies hard. Yet the fact is that all science, and all scholarship, and all art are ideological; there is no neutrality in culture. And the ideology of the education you have just spent four years acquiring in a women's college has been largely, if not entirely, the ideology of white male supremacy, a construct of male subjectivity. The silences, the empty spaces, the language itself, with its excision of the female, the methods of discourse tell us as much as the content, once we learn to watch for what is left out, to listen for the unspoken, to study the patterns of established science and scholarship with an outsider's eye. One of the dangers of a privileged education for women is that we may lose the eye of the outsider and come to believe that those patterns hold for humanity, for the universal, and that they include us.

And so I want to talk today about privilege and about tokenism and about power. Everything I can say to you on this subject comes hard-won, from the lips of a woman privileged by class and skin color, a father's favorite daughter, educated at Radcliffe, which was then casually referred to as the Harvard "Annex." Much of the first four decades of my life was spent in a continuous tension between the world the Fathers taught me to see, and had rewarded me for seeing, and the flashes of insight that came through the eye of the outsider. Gradually those flashes of insight, which at times could seem like brushes with madness, began to demand that I struggle to connect them with each other, to insist that I take them seriously. It was only when I could finally affirm the outsider's eye as the source of a legitimate and coherent vision, that I began to be able to do the work I truly wanted to do, live the kind of life I truly wanted to live, instead of carrying out the assignments

I had been given as a privileged woman and a token. For women, all privilege is relative. Some of you were not born with class or skin-color privilege; but you all have the privilege of education, even if it is an education which has largely denied you knowledge of yourselves as women. You have, to begin with, the privilege of literacy; and it is well for us to remember that, in an age of increasing illiteracy, 60 percent of the world's illiterates are women. Between 1960 and 1970, the number of illiterate men in the world rose by 8 million, while the number of illiterate women rose by 40 million.[1] And the number of illiterate women is increasing. Beyond literacy, you have the privilege of training and tools which can allow you to go beyond the content of your education and re-educate yourselves—to debrief yourselves, we might call it, of the false messages of your education in this culture, the messages telling you that women have not really cared about power or learning or creative opportunities because of a psycho-biological need to serve men and produce children; that only a few atypical women have been exceptions to this rule; the messages telling you that woman's experience is neither normative nor central to human experience. You have the training and the tools to do independent research, to evaluate data, to criticize, and to express in language and visual forms what you discover. This is a privilege, yes, but only if you do not give up in exchange for it the deep knowledge of the unprivileged, the knowledge that, as a woman, you have historically been viewed and still are viewed as existing, not in your own right, but in the service of men. And only if you refuse to give up your capacity to think as a woman, even though in the graduate schools and professions to which many of you will be going you

1. United Nations, Department of International Economic and Social Affairs, Statistical Office, *1977 Compendium of Social Statistics* (New York: United Nations, 1980).

will be praised and rewarded for "thinking like a man."

The word *power* is highly charged for women. It has been long associated for us with the use of force, with rape, with the stockpiling of weapons, with the ruthless accrual of wealth and the hoarding of resources, with the power that acts only in its own interest, despising and exploiting the powerless—including women and children. The effects of this kind of power are all around us, even literally in the water we drink and the air we breathe, in the form of carcinogens and radioactive wastes. But for a long time now, feminists have been talking about redefining power, about that meaning of power which returns to the root—*posse, potere, pouvoir:* to be able, to have the potential, to possess and use one's energy of creation—*transforming power.* An early objection to feminism—in both the nineteenth and twentieth centuries—was that it would make women behave like men—ruthlessly, exploitatively, oppressively. In fact, radical feminism looks to a transformation of human relationships and structures in which power, instead of a thing to be hoarded by a few, would be released to and from within the many, shared in the form of knowledge, expertise, decision making, access to tools, as well as in the basic forms of food and shelter and health care and literacy. Feminists— and many nonfeminists—are, and rightly so, still concerned with what power would mean in such a society, and with the relative differences in power among and between women here and now.

Which brings me to a third meaning of power where women are concerned: the false power which masculine society offers to a few women, on condition that they use it to maintain things as they are, and that they essentially "think like men." This is the meaning of female tokenism: that power withheld from the vast majority of women is offered to a few, so that it appears that any "truly qualified" woman can gain access to leadership, recognition, and reward; hence, that justice based on merit actually prevails. The token woman is encouraged to see herself as different from most other women, as exceptionally talented and deserving, and to separate herself from the wider female condition; and she is perceived by "ordinary" women as separate also, perhaps even as stronger than themselves.

Because you are, within the limits of all women's ultimate outsiderhood, a privileged group of women, it is extremely important for your future sanity that you understand the way tokenism functions. Its most immediate contradiction is that, while it seems to offer the individual token woman a means to realize her creativity, to influence the course of events, it also, by exacting of her certain kinds of behavior and style, acts to blur her outsider's eye, which could be her real source of power and vision. Losing her outsider's vision, she loses the insight which both binds her to other women and affirms her in herself. Tokenism essentially demands that the token deny her identification with women as a group, especially with women less privileged than she: if she is a lesbian, that she deny her relationships with individual women; that she perpetuate rules and structures and criteria and methodologies which have functioned to exclude women; that she renounce or leave undeveloped the critical perspective of her female consciousness. Women unlike herself—poor women, women of color, waitresses, secretaries, housewives in the supermarket, prostitutes, old women—become invisible to her; they may represent too acutely what she has escaped or wished to flee.

President Conway tells me that ever-increasing numbers of you are going on from Smith to medical and law schools. The news, on the face of it, is good: that, thanks to the feminist struggle of the past decade, more doors into these two powerful professions are open to women. I would like to believe that any profession would be better for having more women practicing it, and that any woman practicing law or medicine would use her knowledge and skill to work to transform the realm of health care and the interpretations of the law, to make them responsive to the needs of all those—women, people of color, children, the aged, the dispossessed—for whom they function today as repressive controls. I would like to believe this, but it will not happen even if 50 percent of the members of these professions are women, unless those women refuse to be made into token insiders, unless they zealously preserve the outsider's view and the outsider's consciousness.

For no woman is really an insider in the institutions fathered by masculine consciousness. When we allow ourselves to believe we are, we lose touch with parts of ourselves defined as unacceptable by that consciousness; with the vital toughness and visionary strength of the angry grandmothers, the shamanesses, the fierce marketwomen of the Ibo Women's War, the marriage-resisting women silkworkers of prerevolutionary China, the millions of widows, midwives, and women healers tortured and burned as witches for three centuries in Europe, the Beguines of the twelfth century, who formed independent women's orders outside the domination of the Church, the women of the Paris Commune who marched on Versailles, the uneducated housewives of the Women's Cooperative Guild in England who memorized poetry over the washtub and organized against their oppression as mothers, the women thinkers discredited as "strident," "shrill," "crazy," or "deviant" whose courage to be heretical, to speak their truths, we so badly need to draw upon in our own lives. I believe that every woman's soul is haunted by the spirits of earlier women who fought for their unmet needs and those of their children and their tribes and their peoples, who refused to accept the prescriptions of a male church and state, who took risks and resisted, as women today

—like Inez Garcia, Yvonne Wanrow, Joan Little, Cassandra Peten—are fighting their rapists and batterers. Those spirits dwell in us, trying to speak to us. But we can choose to be deaf; and tokenism, the myth of the "special" woman, the unmothered Athena sprung from her father's brow, can deafen us to their voices.

In this decade now ending, as more women are entering the professions (though still suffering sexual harassment in the workplace, though still, if they have children, carrying two full-time jobs, though still vastly outnumbered by men in upper-level and decision-making jobs), we need most profoundly to remember that early insight of the feminist movement as it evolved in the late sixties: *that no woman is liberated until we all are liberated.* The media flood us with messages to the contrary, telling us that we live in an era when "alternate life styles" are freely accepted, when "marriage contracts" and "the new intimacy" are revolutionizing heterosexual relationships, that shared parenting and the "new fatherhood" will change the world. And we live in a society leeched upon by the "personal growth" and "human potential" industry, by the delusion that individual self-fulfillment can be found in thirteen weeks or a weekend, that the alienation and injustice experienced by women, by Black and Third World people, by the poor, in a world ruled by white males, in a society which fails to meet the most basic needs and which is slowly poisoning itself, can be mitigated or dispersed by Transcendental Meditation. Perhaps the most succinct expression of this message I have seen is the appearance of a magazine for women called *Self.* The insistence of the feminist movement, that each woman's selfhood is precious, that the feminine ethic of self-denial and self-sacrifice must give way to a true woman identification, which would affirm our connectedness with all women, is perverted into a commercially profitable and politically debilitating narcissism. It is important for each of you, toward whom many of these messages are especially directed, to discriminate clearly between "liberated life style" and feminist struggle, and to make a conscious choice.

It's a cliché of commencement speeches that the speaker ends with a peroration telling the new graduates that however badly past generations have behaved, their generation must save the world. I would rather say to you, women of the class of 1979: Try to be worthy of your foresisters, learn from your history, look for inspiration to your ancestresses. If this history has been poorly taught to you, if you do not know it, then use your educational privilege to learn it. Learn how some women of privilege have compromised the greater liberation of women, how others have risked their privileges to further it; learn how brilliant and successful women have failed to create a more just and caring society, precisely because they have tried to do so on terms that the powerful men around them would accept and tolerate. Learn to be worthy of the women of every class, culture, and historical age who did otherwise, who spoke boldly when women were jeered and physically harassed for speaking in public, who—like Anne Hutchinson, Mary Wollstonecraft, the Grimké sisters, Abby Kelley, Ida B. Wells-Barnett, Susan B. Anthony, Lillian Smith, Fannie Lou Hamer —broke taboos, who resisted slavery—their own and other people's. To become a token woman—whether you win the Nobel prize or merely get tenure at the cost of denying your sisters—is to become something less than a man indeed, since men are loyal at least to their own world view, their laws of brotherhood and male self-interest. I am not suggesting that you imitate male loyalties; with the philosopher Mary Daly, I believe that the bonding of women must be utterly different and for an utterly different end: not the misering of resources and power, but the release, in each other, of the yet unexplored

resources and transformative power of women, so long de-
spised, confined, and wasted. Get all the knowledge and skill
you can in whatever professions you enter; but remember that
most of your education must be self-education, in learning the
things women need to know and in calling up the voices we
need to hear within ourselves.

The Problem of
Lorraine Hansberry (1979)

Yes, she is a problem for me, as I read and reread the published
work and some of the unpublished—copies of letters, interview
transcripts, essays. As I listen to her voice on a recording, deep,
young, at twenty-nine, modulated with enormous self-posses-
sion under aggressive cross-examination by Mike Wallace in a
television interview; later the voice becomes a public voice at
once fierce and musical, intense and authoritative. As I read
the explications of her work, her politics, her life and death,
provided in the volumes *To Be Young, Gifted and Black* and
Les Blancs by Robert Nemiroff, James Baldwin, Julius Lester.
As I think of her death at thirty-four from cancer, of the
overwhelming statistics of death by cancer for young Black
women in our time; as I think of the odds against a Black
woman writer surviving at all in this world, finding the life
space in which to work, having her work published or per-
formed, being truly heard or understood. As I reflect on the
stresses of a Black woman trying to write both from "within
the Veil," as she once put it, and for a public which included

This essay was requested by Freedomways *for its special issue on Lorraine
Hansberry,* Art of Thunder, Vision of Light *19, no. 4 (1979), and was first
published there.*

Black women and men, but whose dominant expectations and mythic opinions about the world were shaped by white males; as I think of Broadway, the critics, and the white theatergoing public.[1]

Lorraine Hansberry is a problem to me because she is Black, female, and dead. Her work and her biography have come to us largely through the efforts of her literary executor and divorced husband Robert Nemiroff, who put together both *Les Blancs* (from unfinished manuscripts and notes) and the work which, though it is a collage of her words, is a pattern of his construction: *To Be Young, Gifted and Black.* The problem begins for me when, in reading *Les Blancs,* I do not know when I am reading dialogue written by Hansberry and when I am reading the end product of the process Nemiroff describes:

> After her death, as literary executor, I continued the work: synthesizing the scenes already completed throughout the play with those in progress, drawing upon relevant fragments from earlier drafts, and creating, as needed, dialogue of my own to bridge gaps, deepen relationships or tighten the drama along the lines we had explored together.[2]

All this may be forthright and devoted enough, and it may seem graceless to question the end result.[3] But I do question it, as I question what it means to take *To Be Young, Gifted and Black* as a theater piece by Lorraine Hansberry, let alone

1. *Lorraine Hansberry Speaks Out: Art and the Black Revolution,* selected and ed. Robert Nemiroff (Caedmon recording TC 1352 [1972]).
2. Lorraine Hansberry, *Les Blancs: The Collected Last Plays of Lorraine Hansberry,* ed. Robert Nemiroff (New York: Vintage, 1973), p. 45.
3. It may seem particularly graceless to ask the questions I shall be asking here, since I would not have seen copies of some of the Hansberry documents I shall be using without the kind assistance of Nemiroff, who made them available to me. But to leave my uneasiness unexpressed is, simply, impossible.

any kind of dramatic autobiography. Biography it may be; devoted it may be. But biography by a former husband and literary executor is not the same as autobiography, and Nemiroff acknowledges this.[4] Yet this is the major lens through which Hansberry's life has been viewed. And it is frustrating to me that the Hansberry papers are not simply accessible in an archive open to the public; that students of Black and female history and literature, students of theater, cannot examine freely and draw conclusions about the mass of material from which *To Be Young, Gifted and Black* was sifted and selected, the drafts and notes from which the final version of *Les Blancs* was posthumously edited.

I wish to address the life/work of Lorraine Hansberry from a woman's perspective, a feminist perspective, within the limitations of my experience as a white woman. I cannot assume knowledge of what the characters Beneatha and Ruth would have meant to a young Black woman student, or married woman, in 1959; what Lena Younger would have meant to an older Black woman in the theater audiences of that year. But as a feminist critic, my concern is not only to read the work of past and present women writers with a woman-identified perspective; it is to help create more possibilities for women writers in the future. My task, therefore, is to comprehend how the political meaning of being a woman shapes and affects both substance and form in women's art; what interruptions, silences, resistances, censorships confront a woman artist working in a dominant culture which derogates both the female body and female creativity. A decade of white feminist criticism has taught us much about the circumstances under which

4. Lorraine Hansberry, *To Be Young, Gifted and Black: Lorraine Hansberry in Her Own Words,* adapt. Robert Nemiroff (New York: Signet, 1969), p. xxii.

women have written, much about the struggles and choices involved in getting that writing read. But within white feminist criticism itself there have been notable silences, erasures. The Black woman writer, as Barbara Smith has noted, suffers from a double erasure:

> When Black women's books are dealt with at all, it is usually in the context of Black literature which largely ignores the implications of sexual politics. When white women look at Black women's works they are of course ill-equipped to deal with the subtleties of racial politics.[5]

To read Lorraine Hansberry, to understand the meaning of her work, means for me of necessity to question all filters, all "translations"; to view the work in the context of what it means to be both Black and female in a world where each is a stigmatized or an erased identity. I cannot afford the luxury of an unexamined "humanism," a position defined and ordered by white males; no more can I accept any male judgment as to the intrinsic radicalism of any woman, Black or white.

Lorraine Hansberry is a problem to me, then, because even as I read *A Raisin in the Sun* I am aware of the inner and outer contradictions spawned when a writer who is both Black and female tries with passionate intent to make a statement which can be heard by those who are neither, and tries specifically to get that statement heard in the Broadway theater—a theater that is commercial and capitalist in the extreme. Of even the blandest, most digestible plays, we know that hands other than the playwright's have snipped and smoothed, pried apart and reglued the original script with an eye to making back the

5. Barbara Smith, "Toward a Black Feminist Criticism," in *All the Women Are White, All the Blacks Are Men, but Some of Us Are Brave: Black Women's Studies*, ed. Gloria T. Hull, Patricia Bell Scott, and Barbara Smith (Old Westbury, N.Y.: Feminist Press, 1982).

investment, following those economics of the New York thea-
ter which Nemiroff himself has described.[6] But even be-
fore that process begins, I know from my own experience as a
white, lesbian, feminist writer that the first—and last—
censors are interior when we are writing in the face of that
judgment and culture of white males, that cultural jury which
presumes to set standards, to determine whose experience
counts, which themes are "universal" and which "paro-
chial," to define the literary canon, to define "greatness" it-
self. I cannot attempt here to explore where or how this bril-
liant, ardent, and very angry woman may have encountered
both interior and exterior censors. But a few clues are avail-
able, and they fascinate me.

For example, according to Nemiroff's "Critical Back-
ground" to *Les Blancs*, in Hansberry's earliest notes for the
play, made in 1960, she conceived of an African woman, Can-
dace, returning to her tribal village *for her mother's funeral*—
a daughter and a mother who apparently became transformed
into the intellectual, Europeanized Tshembe and his father,
the dead Kwi warrior. Lorraine Hansberry was a student of
African history and culture long before the invention of Black
Studies and was surely aware of the powerful woman-to-woman
bonding in tribal societies, aware of the exercise of economic
and political power by African women. But in the existing
version of the play there is no African woman, only a vision of
the Dancer in the sky. In September of the same year, Hans-
berry listed among her future projects a musical drama to be
entitled *The Sign in Jenny Reed's Window.* (When—why—
did Candace become metamorphosed into Tshembe, Jenny
Reed into Sidney Brustein?) In the same list of "proposed

6. Robert Nemiroff, "The 101 'Final' Performances of *Sidney Brustein,*" in Lorraine
Hansberry, *A Raisin in the Sun/The Sign in Sidney Brustein's Window* (New York:
Signet, 1966), pp. 151–152.

work" appears the note *"The Life of Mary Wollstonecraft,* full length drama."[7]

She was, it is clear, an early and lucid feminist. In 1957, she had begun the draft of an essay on Simone de Beauvoir's *The Second Sex* in which Hansberry said, *"The Second Sex* may well be the most important work of this century." She assessed the reception of the book in America, the gossip surrounding de Beauvoir's personal life which substituted for serious debate on her ideas. In the course of this essay, she addressed the politics of housework, pornography (which she recognized immediately as a feminist issue), women's work outside the home, the politics of dress and adornment, the socialist position regarding women's role, and much else that the late 1960s wave of feminism was to address as if for the first time.[8] In 1961, she wrote an essay ironically entitled "In Defense of the Equality of *Men"* in which she challenged psychoanalytic theories of femaleness and, long before a movement for battered women existed, wrote:

> In a widely read women's magazine in a feature called "Making Marriage Work" the professor-analyst tackled what might seem to the excessively civilized a resolved question: "Should A Husband Strike His Wife?" Bending to enlightenment, the writer opined, "It is impossible to condone such behavior." He then went on, however, to modify that bit of radical abandon by advising his readers that the "provocation" by wives was undoubtedly far greater than they realized. He offered the following directions to wives as to how best to avoid their partially deserved beatings: "Gauge his mood; avoid arguments; indulge his whims; help him relax; keep love alive."

7. Robert Nemiroff, "A Critical Background," in Hansberry, *Les Blancs,* p. 41; Hansberry, *To Be Young, Gifted and Black,* p. 137.

8. Lorraine Hansberry, "Simone de Beauvoir and *The Second Sex:* An American Commentary 1957," unpub. ms.

In the same essay, she challenges the myth that American women tyrannize over "the home and even the wealth of the nation." She also quotes Susan B. Anthony and, again, takes up the issue of pornography along with that of censorship.[9] Much earlier, at the age of twenty-five, in a letter to the newly founded *Village Voice,* Hansberry had protested a laudatory review of Strindberg's *Comrades* on the ground that

> the playwright clearly hated women. . . . It is probably true that if the play had had a reverse point of view that it might have been dismissed rapidly as a badly-written piece of "Feminist" *propaganda.* Sometimes it almost seems that only when propaganda is propagandizing a return to a dead and useless past is it profound, —"art"/avant-garde, etc. . . . there have been, as of yet, too many Strindbergs (in one degree or another) and too few Ibsens and Shaws. . . . The only answer, in drama, to Bertha Alberg is Nora Helmer.[10]

Did Lorraine Hansberry ever conceive of Candace or Jenny Reed or Mary Wollstonecraft as her answer, in drama, to Bertha Alberg? Did she think of Lena Younger in those terms? In an address to the American Academy of Psycho-Therapists in 1963, Hansberry, speaking to the followers of Freud, says of the maligned and sentimentalized "Black matriarch":

> It is she who, while seeming to cling to traditional restraints, drives the young on into the fire hoses and one day simply refuses to move to the back of the bus in Montgomery, or goes out and buys a house in an all-white community where her fourth child and sec-

9. Lorraine Hansberry, "In Defense of the Equality of *Men,*" in *The Norton Anthology of Literature by Women,* ed. Sandra M. Gilbert and Susan Gubar (New York: W. W. Norton, 1985), pp. 2061, 2063.

10. Lorraine Hansberry, "On Strindberg and Sexism," in Karen Malpede, *Women in Theatre: Compassion & Hope* (New York: Drama Book Publisher, 1983, and Limelight Editions, 1985), pp. 171–173.

ond daughter will almost be killed by a brick thrown through the window by a shrieking racist mob.[11]

She was thinking of her own mother, presumably, but also of Lena Younger. Yet those unpublished and fragmentary clues suggest a Black feminist anger which is less clearly reflected by the depiction of women in her plays. The women in *A Raisin in the Sun* and *Sidney Brustein* flash at moments with this anger, but it is Lena's son, Walter Lee, who finally is given the *dramaturgic* confrontation with the envoy from the racist neighborhood. It is Hannibal, in *The Drinking Gourd*, her unproduced television play, who dares to plot escape, who learns to read and is blinded for so doing. And there is no actual, flesh-and-blood African woman in *Les Blancs* as we have it.

Yet Hansberry said clearly, in an interview with Studs Terkel in 1959:

> Obviously the most oppressed of any oppressed group will be its women. . . . Obviously, since women, period are oppressed in society, and if you've got an oppressed group, they're *twice* oppressed. So I should imagine that they react accordingly: As oppression makes people more militant . . . then *twice* militant, because they're *twice oppressed.* So that there's an assumption of leadership historically.[12]

In light of this comment, I find the question of Lorraine Hansberry's female characters—their position in the plays— worth pondering. Could the American, largely white, theater-

11. From "Origins of Character," address to the American Academy of Psycho-Therapists, October 5, 1963, excerpted by Robert Nemiroff for a typescript entitled "Lorraine Hansberry on—Mama."

12. From "An Interview with Lorraine Hansberry by Studs Terkel," May 12, 1959, recorded at 1145 Hyde Park Boulevard, Chicago. Six pages from this interview are reprinted in *American Theatre* 1, no. 7 (November 1984).

going public of the 1950s and early 1960s have accepted as a central character a female revolutionary, a confrontational figure, a strong Black woman who was not Mama, who was, let us say, both angry and sexual, who could be seen moving into a more radical position as Walter Lee Younger and Sidney Brustein are seen moving as the play progresses? Could such a Black heroine—one who was "twice militant," a leader, an Ida B. Wells or a Fannie Lou Hamer—gain exposure on the Broadway stage or television screen in 1979?

Hansberry also wrote several letters to the early lesbian publication *The Ladder* in 1957 on the economic and psychological pressures that impel many conscious lesbians into marriage, on the connections between anti-homosexuality and anti-feminism, and on the need for a new, *feminist* ethics.[13] I find myself wondering who were the women friends with whom she discussed *The Second Sex?* Who were the women she seems to be trying to reach in her unfinished essay on that book? In their book *Lesbian/Woman,* Del Martin and Phyllis Lyon remark, "Many Black women who had been involved in the homophile movement found themselves forced to make a choice between two 'Causes' that touched their lives so intimately. One of them wrote a play that was a hit on Broadway."[14] What does this tell us about the possible censorship, self-imposed and external, that had to be confronted by the author of *A Raisin in the Sun?*

So many of the truths of women's lives, so much of women's writing, have come to us in fragments, over time, that for

13. See Jonathan Katz, ed., *Gay American History: Lesbians and Gay Men in the U.S.A.* (New York: Thomas Y. Crowell, 1976), p. 425. I am indebted to Barbara Grier for providing me with copies of the fuller versions of these letters (signed L.H.N., New York, N.Y., and L.N., New York, N.Y.) as published in *The Ladder* 1, nos. 8 and 11 (May and August 1957).

14. Del Martin and Phyllis Lyon, *Lesbian/Woman* (New York: Bantam, 1972), p. 122.

decades their work is half-understood and we have only clues as to their real stature. I think of Emily Dickinson, published for half a century in smoothed-out, tidied versions, her full power revealed only years after her death; of Virginia Woolf, labeled ''Bloomsbury,'' elitist, and mentally unstable, her political radicalism, class consciousness, and lesbianism erased or veiled by her husband's editing, coming fully to light only within the last two or three years; of Zora Neale Hurston, whose life and work, despite Robert Hemenway's exhaustive biography, have yet to be examined in depth from a Black female perspective, though both Alice Walker and Lorraine Bethel have begun to do this.[15] Lorraine Hansberry, charged by critics, on the one hand, with having created a reactionary Black "mammy" in Lena Younger and, on the other, with advocating genocide against whites, deserves similar scrutiny. How ironic that she would come to be dismissed contemptuously by some as a liberal when she had written as early as 1962:

> I think, then, that Negroes must concern themselves with every single means of struggle: legal, illegal, passive, active, violent and non-violent. . . . They must harass, debate, petition, boycott, sing hymns, pray on steps—and shoot from their windows when the racists come cruising through their communities. . . . The acceptance of our condition is the only form of extremism which discredits us before our children.[16]

And as early as 1957:

15. See "In Search of Zora Neale Hurston," in Alice Walker, *In Search of Our Mothers' Gardens* (New York: Harcourt, Brace, Jovanovich, 1983), pp. 83–116; also Walker's foreword to Robert Hemenway, *Zora Neale Hurston: A Literary Biography* (Champaign: University of Illinois Press, 1977). See also Lorraine Bethel, " 'This Infinity of Conscious Pain': Zora Neale Hurston and the Black Female Literary Tradition," in Hull, Scott, and Smith, pp. 176–189.
16. Hansberry, *To Be Young, Gifted and Black*, p. 222.

Woman like the Negro, like the Jew, like colonial peoples, even in ignorance, is *incapable of accepting the role with harmony.* This is because it is an unnatural role. . . . The station of woman is hardly one that she would assume by choice, any more than men would. It must necessarily be imposed on her—by force. . . . A status not freely chosen or entered into by an individual or group is necessarily one of oppression and the oppressed are by their nature . . . forever in ferment and agitation against their condition and what they understand to be their oppressors. If not by overt rebellion or revolution, then in the thousand and one ways they will devise with and without consciousness to alter their condition.[17]

What, then, were Lorraine Hansberry's conscious and unconscious conflicts and choices when, as a Black woman, she sought to write plays which stood any chance of being heard on the American stage? What did she dream of being free to write should she gain validation from the American white male establishment? What did it mean to be one of the tiny handful of Black women artists who have found it possible to have their works published, performed, or seen? What was the community, what was the loneliness, from within which she worked? It seems to me impossible to talk about what is presently visible of Lorraine Hansberry's writings without asking questions like these. Did she know, had she read, Zora Neale Hurston? What Black women writers did she read? Had she read the white anti-racist southern writer Lillian Smith, who also wrote from a female consciousness?

And these questions flow into others for me—unanswerable questions, unprovable hypotheses, yet irresistible in this time and place. Where would Hansberry have placed herself, had she lived till now, in relation to the feminist movement of the present? How would she have responded to the poetry of June

17. Hansberry, "Simone de Beauvoir."

Jordan, to a Black feminist manifesto such as the Combahee River Collective statement,[18] to Alice Walker's "In Search of Our Mothers' Gardens"[19] and *Meridian*, to Audre Lorde's *The Black Unicorn* or "Scratching the Surface";[20] to the music of Bernice Reagon, Mary Watkins, Linda Tillery; to Ntozake Shange's *For Colored Girls Who Have Considered Suicide* . . . ? What would she have made of Barbara Smith's declaration that "I want most of all for Black women and Black lesbians somehow not to be so alone. This . . . will require the most expansive of revolutions as well as many new words to tell us how to make this revolution real"?[21]

I cannot presume to have answers to these questions. Lorraine Hansberry remains a problem and a challenge. I wait for the Black feminist who, with free access to Hansberry's unpublished papers, can help us see her unidealized, unsimplified, in her fullest complexity, in her fullest political context. I do know that fame and economic security are not enough to enable the woman artist—Black or white—to push her art and thought to their outermost limits. For that, we need community—a community whose members know our experience from the inside out because it is their own, who will support us in our efforts to depict that experience in the face of those who would either reward us for glossing over, or punish us for articulating, the extremity in which we live.

18. "The Combahee River Collective: A Black Feminist Statement," in *Capitalist Patriarchy and the Case for Socialist Feminism*, ed. Zillah Eisenstein (New York: Monthly Review Press, 1979). See also Barbara Smith, ed., *Home Girls: A Black Feminist Anthology* (New York: Kitchen Table/Women of Color Press, 1983), pp. 272–282.

19. In Pamela Daniels and Sara Ruddick, eds., *Working It Out* (New York: Pantheon, 1977).

20. Audre Lorde, *The Black Unicorn* (New York: W. W. Norton, 1978). Audre Lorde, "Scratching the Surface: Some Notes on Barriers to Women and Loving," *The Black Scholar* 9, no. 7 (April 1978).

21. Hull, Scott and Smith, p. 173.

Compulsory Heterosexuality and Lesbian Existence (1980)

FOREWORD

I want to say a little about the way "Compulsory Hetero-sexuality" was originally conceived and the context in which we are now living. It was written in part to chal-lenge the erasure of lesbian existence from so much of scholarly feminist literature, an erasure which I felt (and feel) to be not just anti-lesbian, but anti-feminist in its consequences, and to distort the experience of heterosexual women as well. It was not written to widen divisions but to encourage heterosexual feminists to examine heterosexu-ality as a political institution which disempowers women— and to change it. I also hoped that other lesbians would feel the depth and breadth of woman identification and woman bonding that has run like a continuous though stifled theme through the heterosexual experience, and that this would become increasingly a politically activating impulse, not simply a validation of personal lives. I wanted the essay to suggest new kinds of criticism, to incite new questions in classrooms and academic journals, and to

Orginally written in 1978 for the "Sexuality" issue of Signs, *this essay was published there in 1980. In 1982 Antelope Publications reprinted it as part of a feminist pamphlet series. The foreword was written for the pamphlet.*

sketch, at least, some bridge over the gap between *lesbian* and *feminist.* I wanted, at the very least, for feminists to find it less possible to read, write, or teach from a perspective of unexamined heterocentricity.

Within the three years since I wrote "Compulsory Heterosexuality"—with this energy of hope and desire—the pressures to conform in a society increasingly conservative in mood have become more intense. The New Right's messages to women have been, precisely, that we are the emotional and sexual property of men, and that the autonomy and equality of women threaten family, religion, and state. The institutions by which women have traditionally been controlled—patriarchal motherhood, economic exploitation, the nuclear family, compulsory heterosexuality—are being strengthened by legislation, religious fiat, media imagery, and efforts at censorship. In a worsening economy, the single mother trying to support her children confronts the feminization of poverty which Joyce Miller of the National Coalition of Labor Union Women has named one of the major issues of the 1980s. The lesbian, unless in disguise, faces discrimination in hiring and harassment and violence in the street. Even within feminist-inspired institutions such as battered-women's shelters and Women's Studies programs, open lesbians are fired and others warned to stay in the closet. The retreat into sameness—assimilation for those who can manage it—is the most passive and debilitating of responses to political repression, economic insecurity, and a renewed open season on difference.

I want to note that documentation of male violence against women—within the home especially—has been accumulating rapidly in this period (see pages 30–31, note 9). At the same time, in the realm of literature which depicts woman bonding and woman identification as essential for female survival, a steady stream of writing and criticism has been coming from women of color in general and lesbians of color in particular—the latter group being even more profoundly erased in academic feminist scholarship by the double bias of racism and homophobia.[1]

There has recently been an intensified debate on female sexuality among feminists and lesbians, with lines often furiously and bitterly drawn, with *sadomasochism* and *pornography* as key words which are variously defined according to who is talking. The depth of women's rage and fear regarding sexuality and its relation to power and pain is real, even when the dialogue sounds simplistic, self-righteous, or like parallel monologues.

Because of all these developments, there are parts of this essay that I would word differently, qualify, or expand if I were writing it today. But I continue to think that heterosexual feminists will draw political strength for change from taking a critical stance toward the ideology which *demands* heterosexuality, and that lesbians cannot assume that we are untouched by that ideology and the institutions founded

1. See, for example, Paula Gunn Allen, *The Sacred Hoop: Recovering the Feminine in American Indian Traditions* (Boston: Beacon, 1986); Beth Brant, ed., *A Gathering of Spirit: Writing and Art by North American Indian Women* (Montpelier, Vt.: Sinister Wisdom Books, 1984); Gloria Anzaldúa and Cherríe Moraga, eds., *This Bridge Called My Back: Writings by Radical Women of Color* (Watertown, Mass.: Persephone, 1981; distributed by Kitchen Table/Women of Color Press, Albany, N.Y.); J. R. Roberts, *Black Lesbians: An Annotated Bibliography* (Tallahassee, Fla.: Naiad, 1981); Barbara Smith, ed., *Home Girls: A Black Feminist Anthology* (Albany, N.Y.: Kitchen Table/Women of Color Press, 1984). As Lorraine Bethel and Barbara Smith pointed out in *Conditions 5: The Black Women's Issue* (1980), a great deal of fiction by Black women depicts primary relationships between women. I would like to cite here the work of Ama Ata Aidoo, Toni Cade Bambara, Buchi Emecheta, Bessie Head, Zora Neale Hurston, Alice Walker. Donna Allegra, Red Jordan Arobateau, Audre Lorde, Ann Allen Shockley, among others, write directly as Black lesbians. For fiction by other lesbians of color, see Elly Bulkin, ed., *Lesbian Fiction: An Anthology* (Watertown, Mass.: Persephone, 1981).

See also, for accounts of contemporary Jewish-lesbian existence, Evelyn Torton Beck, ed., *Nice Jewish Girls: A Lesbian Anthology* (Watertown, Mass.: Persephone, 1982; distributed by Crossing Press, Trumansburg, N.Y. 14886); Alice Bloch, *Lifetime Guarantee* (Watertown, Mass.: Persephone, 1982); and Melanie Kaye-Kantrowitz and Irena Klepfisz, eds., *The Tribe of Dina: A Jewish Women's Anthology* (Montpelier, Vt.: Sinister Wisdom Books, 1986).

The earliest formulation that I know of heterosexuality as an institution was in the lesbian-feminist paper *The Furies*, founded in 1971. For a collection of articles from that paper, see Nancy Myron and Charlotte Bunch, eds., *Lesbianism and the Women's Movement* (Oakland, Calif.: Diana Press, 1975; distributed by Crossing Press, Trumansburg, N.Y. 14886).

upon it. There is nothing about such a critique that requires us to think of ourselves as victims, as having been brainwashed or totally powerless. Coercion and compulsion are among the conditions in which women have learned to recognize our strength. Resistance is a major theme in this essay and in the study of women's lives, if we know what we are looking for.

I

Biologically men have only one innate orientation—a sexual one that draws them to women,—while women have two innate orientations, sexual toward men and reproductive toward their young.[2]

I was a woman terribly vulnerable, critical, using femaleness as a sort of standard or yardstick to measure and discard men. Yes—something like that. I was an Anna who invited defeat from men without ever being conscious of it. (But I am conscious of it. And being conscious of it means I shall leave it all behind me and become—but what?) I was stuck fast in an emotion common to women of our time, that can turn them bitter, or Lesbian, or solitary. Yes, that Anna during that time was . . .

[Another blank line across the page:][3]

The bias of compulsory heterosexuality, through which lesbian experience is perceived on a scale ranging from deviant to abhorrent or simply rendered invisible, could be illustrated from many texts other than the two just preceding. The assumption made by Rossi, that women are "innately" sexually oriented only toward men, and that made by Lessing, that the

---

2. Alice Rossi, "Children and Work in the Lives of Women," paper delivered at the University of Arizona, Tuscon, February 1976.
3. Doris Lessing, *The Golden Notebook*, 1962 (New York: Bantam, 1977), p. 480.

lesbian is simply acting out of her bitterness toward men, are by no means theirs alone; these assumptions are widely current in literature and in the social sciences.

I am concerned here with two other matters as well: first, how and why women's choice of women as passionate comrades, life partners, co-workers, lovers, community has been crushed, invalidated, forced into hiding and disguise; and second, the virtual or total neglect of lesbian existence in a wide range of writings, including feminist scholarship. Obviously there is a connection here. I believe that much feminist theory and criticism is stranded on this shoal.

My organizing impulse is the belief that it is not enough for feminist thought that specifically lesbian texts exist. Any theory or cultural/political creation that treats lesbian existence as a marginal or less "natural" phenomenon, as mere "sexual preference," or as the mirror image of either heterosexual or male homosexual relations is profoundly weakened thereby, whatever its other contributions. Feminist theory can no longer afford merely to voice a toleration of "lesbianism" as an "alternative life style" or make token allusion to lesbians. A feminist critique of compulsory heterosexual orientation for women is long overdue. In this exploratory paper, I shall try to show why.

I will begin by way of examples, briefly discussing four books that have appeared in the last few years, written from different viewpoints and political orientations, but all presenting themselves, and favorably reviewed, as feminist.[4] All take as a basic assumption that the social relations of the sexes are disordered

4. Nancy Chodorow, *The Reproduction of Mothering* (Berkeley: University of California Press, 1978); Dorothy Dinnerstein, *The Mermaid and the Minotaur: Sexual Arrangements and the Human Malaise* (New York: Harper & Row, 1976); Barbara Ehrenreich and Deirdre English, *For Her Own Good: 150 Years of the Experts' Advice to Women* (Garden City, N.Y.: Doubleday, Anchor, 1978); Jean Baker Miller, *Toward a New Psychology of Women* (Boston: Beacon, 1976).

and extremely problematic, if not disabling, for women; all seek paths toward change. I have learned more from some of these books than from others, but on this I am clear: each one might have been more accurate, more powerful, more truly a force for change had the author dealt with lesbian existence as a reality and as a source of knowledge and power available to women, or with the institution of heterosexuality itself as a beachhead of male dominance.[5] In none of them is the question ever raised as to whether, in a different context or other things being equal, women would *choose* heterosexual coupling and marriage; heterosexuality is presumed the "sexual preference" of "most women," either implicitly or explicitly. In none of these books, which concern themselves with mothering, sex roles, relationships, and societal prescriptions for women, is compul-

5. I could have chosen many other serious and influential recent books, including anthologies, which would illustrate the same point: e.g., *Our Bodies, Ourselves,* the Boston Women's Health Book Collective's best seller (New York: Simon and Schuster, 1976), which devotes a separate (and inadequate) chapter to lesbians, but whose message is that heterosexuality is most women's life preference; Berenice Carroll, ed., *Liberating Women's History: Theoretical and Critical Essays* (Urbana: University of Illinois Press, 1976), which does not include even a token essay on the lesbian presence in history, though an essay by Linda Gordon, Persis Hunt, *et al.* notes the use by male historians of "sexual deviance" as a category to discredit and dismiss Anna Howard Shaw, Jane Addams, and other feminists ("Historical Phallacies: Sexism in American Historical Writing"); and Renate Bridenthal and Claudia Koonz, eds., *Becoming Visible: Women in European History* (Boston: Houghton Mifflin, 1977), which contains three mentions of male homosexuality but no materials that I have been able to locate on lesbians. Gerda Lerner, ed., *The Female Experience: An American Documentary* (Indianapolis: Bobbs-Merrill, 1977), contains an abridgment of two lesbian-feminist–position papers from the contemporary movement but no other documentation of lesbian existence. Lerner does note in her preface, however, how the charge of deviance has been used to fragment women and discourage women's resistance. Linda Gordon, in *Woman's Body, Woman's Right: A Social History of Birth Control in America* (New York: Viking, Grossman, 1976), notes accurately that "it is not that feminism has produced more lesbians. There have always been many lesbians, despite the high levels of repression; and most lesbians experience their sexual preference as innate" (p. 410).

[A.R., 1986: I am glad to update the first annotation in this footnote. *"The New" Our Bodies, Ourselves* (New York: Simon and Schuster, 1984) contains an expanded chapter on "Loving Women: Lesbian Life and Relationships" and furthermore emphasizes *choices* for women throughout—in terms of sexuality, health care, family, politics, etc.]

sory heterosexuality ever examined as an institution powerfully affecting all these, or the idea of "preference" or "innate orientation" even indirectly questioned.

In *For Her Own Good: 150 Years of the Experts' Advice to Women* by Barbara Ehrenreich and Deirdre English, the authors' superb pamphlets *Witches, Midwives and Nurses: A History of Women Healers* and *Complaints and Disorders: The Sexual Politics of Sickness* are developed into a provocative and complex study. Their thesis in this book is that the advice given to American women by male health professionals, particularly in the areas of marital sex, maternity, and child care, has echoed the dictates of the economic marketplace and the role capitalism has needed women to play in production and/or reproduction. Women have become the consumer victims of various cures, therapies, and normative judgments in different periods (including the prescription to middle-class women to embody and preserve the sacredness of the home—the "scientific" romanticization of the home itself). None of the "experts' " advice has been either particularly scientific or women-oriented; it has reflected male needs, male fantasies about women, and male interest in controlling women—particularly in the realms of sexuality and motherhood—fused with the requirements of industrial capitalism. So much of this book is so devastatingly informative and is written with such lucid feminist wit, that I kept waiting as I read for the basic proscription against lesbianism to be examined. It never was.

This can hardly be for lack of information. Jonathan Katz's *Gay American History*[6] tells us that as early as 1656 the New Haven Colony prescribed the death penalty for lesbians. Katz provides many suggestive and informative documents on the

---

6. Jonathan Katz, ed., *Gay American History: Lesbians and Gay Men in the U.S.A.* (New York: Thomas Y. Crowell, 1976).

"treatment" (or torture) of lesbians by the medical profession in the nineteenth and twentieth centuries. Recent work by the historian Nancy Sahli documents the crackdown on intense female friendships among college women at the turn of the present century.[7] The ironic title *For Her Own Good* might have referred first and foremost to the economic imperative to heterosexuality and marriage and to the sanctions imposed against single women and widows—both of whom have been and still are viewed as deviant. Yet, in this often enlightening Marxist-feminist overview of male prescriptions for female sanity and health, the economics of prescriptive heterosexuality go unexamined.[8]

Of the three psychoanalytically based books, one, Jean Baker Miller's *Toward a New Psychology of Women,* is written as if lesbians simply do not exist, even as marginal beings. Given Miller's title, I find this astonishing. However, the favorable reviews the book has received in feminist journals, including *Signs* and *Spokeswoman,* suggest that Miller's heterocentric assumptions are widely shared. In *The Mermaid and the Minotaur: Sexual Arrangements and the Human Malaise,* Dorothy Dinnerstein makes an impassioned argument for the sharing of parenting between women and men and for an end to what she perceives as the male/female symbiosis of "gender arrangements," which she feels are leading the species further and further into violence and self-extinction. Apart from other problems that I have with this book (including her silence on the institutional and random terrorism men have practiced on women—and children—throughout history,[9] and her obses-

7. Nancy Sahli, "Smashing Women's Relationships before the Fall," *Chrysalis: A Magazine of Women's Culture* 8 (1979): 17–27.

8. This is a book which I have publicly endorsed. I would still do so, though with the above caveat. It is only since beginning to write this article that I fully appreciated how enormous is the unasked question in Ehrenreich and English's book.

9. See, for example, Kathleen Barry, *Female Sexual Slavery* (Englewood Cliffs, N.J.: Prentice-Hall, 1979); Mary Daly, *Gyn/Ecology: The Metaethics of Radical Feminism*

sion with psychology to the neglect of economic and other material realities that help to create psychological reality), I find Dinnerstein's view of the relations between women and men as "a collaboration to keep history mad" utterly ahistorical. She means by this a collaboration to perpetuate social relations which are hostile, exploitative, and destructive to life itself. She sees women and men as equal partners in the making of "sexual arrangements," seemingly unaware of the repeated struggles of women to resist oppression (their own and that of others) and to change their condition. She ignores, specifically, the history of women who—as witches, *femmes seules,* marriage resisters, spinsters, autonomous widows, and/or lesbians —have managed on varying levels *not* to collaborate. It is this history, precisely, from which feminists have so much to learn and on which there is overall such blanketing silence. Dinnerstein acknowledges at the end of her book that "female separatism," though "on a large scale and in the long run wildly impractical," has something to teach us: "Separate, women could in principle set out to learn from scratch—undeflected by the opportunities to evade this task that men's presence has

---

(Boston: Beacon, 1978); Susan Griffin, *Woman and Nature: The Roaring inside Her* (New York: Harper & Row, 1978); Diana Russell and Nicole van de Ven, eds., *Proceedings of the International Tribunal of Crimes against Women* (Millbrae, Calif.: Les Femmes, 1976); and Susan Brownmiller, *Against Our Will: Men, Women and Rape* (New York: Simon and Schuster, 1975); *Aegis: Magazine on Ending Violence against Women* (Feminist Alliance against Rape, P.O. Box 21033, Washington, D.C. 20009).

[A.R., 1986: Work on both incest and on woman battering has appeared in the 1980s which I did not cite in the essay. See Florence Rush, *The Best-kept Secret* (New York: McGraw-Hill, 1980); Louise Armstrong, *Kiss Daddy Goodnight: A Speakout on Incest* (New York: Pocket Books, 1979); Sandra Butler, *Conspiracy of Silence: The Trauma of Incest* (San Francisco: New Glide, 1978); F. Delacoste and F. Newman, eds., *Fight Back!: Feminist Resistance to Male Violence* (Minneapolis: Cleis Press, 1981); Judy Freespirit, *Daddy's Girl: An Incest Survivor's Story* (Langlois, Ore.: Diaspora Distribution, 1982); Judith Herman, *Father-Daughter Incest* (Cambridge, Mass.: Harvard University Press, 1981); Toni McNaron and Yarrow Morgan, eds., *Voices in the Night: Women Speaking about Incest* (Minneapolis: Cleis Press, 1982); and Betsy Warrior's richly informative, multipurpose compilation of essays, statistics, listings, and facts, the *Battered Women's Directory* (formerly entitled *Working on Wife Abuse*), 8th ed. (Cambridge, Mass.: 1982).]

so far offered—what intact self-creative humanness is."[10]
Phrases like "intact self-creative humanness" obscure the question of what the many forms of female separatism have actually been addressing. The fact is that women in every culture and throughout history *have* undertaken the task of independent, nonheterosexual, woman-connected existence, to the extent made possible by their context, often in the belief that they were the "only ones" ever to have done so. They have undertaken it even though few women have been in an economic position to resist marriage altogether, and even though attacks against unmarried women have ranged from aspersion and mockery to deliberate gynocide, including the burning and torturing of millions of widows and spinsters during the witch persecutions of the fifteenth, sixteenth, and seventeenth centuries in Europe.

Nancy Chodorow does come close to the edge of an acknowledgment of lesbian existence. Like Dinnerstein, Chodorow believes that the fact that women, and women only, are responsible for child care in the sexual division of labor has led to an entire social organization of gender inequality, and that men as well as women must become primary carers for children if that inequality is to change. In the process of examining, from a psychoanalytic perspective, how mothering by women affects the psychological development of girl and boy children, she offers documentation that men are "emotionally secondary" in women's lives, that "women have a richer, ongoing inner world to fall back on . . . men do not become as emotionally important to women as women do to men."[11] This would carry into the late twentieth century Smith-Rosenberg's findings about eighteenth- and nineteenth-century women's

10. Dinnerstein, p. 272.
11. Chodorow, pp. 197–198.

emotional focus on women. "Emotionally important" can, of course, refer to anger as well as to love, or to that intense mixture of the two often found in women's relationships with women—one aspect of what I have come to call the "double life of women" (see below). Chodorow concludes that because women have women as mothers, "the mother remains a primary internal object [*sic*] to the girl, so that heterosexual relationships are on the model of a nonexclusive, second relationship for her, whereas for the boy they re-create an exclusive, primary relationship." According to Chodorow, women "have learned to deny the limitations of masculine lovers for both psychological and practical reasons."[12]

But the practical reasons (like witch burnings, male control of law, theology, and science, or economic nonviability within the sexual division of labor) are glossed over. Chodorow's account barely glances at the constraints and sanctions which historically have enforced or ensured the coupling of women with men and obstructed or penalized women's coupling or allying in independent groups with other women. She dismisses lesbian existence with the comment that "lesbian relationships do tend to re-create mother-daughter emotions and connections, but most women are heterosexual" (implied: more mature, having developed beyond the mother-daughter connection?). She then adds: "This heterosexual preference and taboos on homosexuality, in addition to objective economic dependence on men, make the option of primary sexual bonds with other women unlikely—though more prevalent in recent years."[13] The significance of that qualification seems irresistible, but Chodorow does not explore it further. Is she saying that lesbian existence has become more *visible* in recent years

12. *Ibid.*, pp. 198–199.
13. *Ibid.*, p. 200.

(in certain groups), that economic and other pressures have changed (under capitalism, socialism, or both), and that consequently more women are rejecting the heterosexual "choice"? She argues that women want children because their heterosexual relationships lack richness and intensity, that in having a child a woman seeks to re-create her own intense relationship with her mother. It seems to me that on the basis of her own findings, Chodorow leads us implicitly to conclude that heterosexuality is *not* a "preference" for women, that, for one thing, it fragments the erotic from the emotional in a way that women find impoverishing and painful. Yet her book participates in mandating it. Neglecting the covert socializations and the overt forces which have channeled women into marriage and heterosexual romance, pressures ranging from the selling of daughters to the silences of literature to the images of the television screen, she, like Dinnerstein, is stuck with trying to reform a man-made institution—compulsory heterosexuality— as if, despite profound emotional impulses and complementarities drawing women toward women, there is a mystical/biological heterosexual inclination, a "preference" or "choice" which draws women toward men.

Moreover, it is understood that this "preference" does not need to be explained unless through the tortuous theory of the female Oedipus complex or the necessity for species reproduction. It is lesbian sexuality which (usually, and incorrectly, "included" under male homosexuality) is seen as requiring explanation. This assumption of female heterosexuality seems to me in itself remarkable: it is an enormous assumption to have glided so silently into the foundations of our thought.

The extension of this assumption is the frequently heard assertion that in a world of genuine equality, where men are nonoppressive and nurturing, everyone would be bisexual. Such a notion blurs and sentimentalizes the actualities within which women have experienced sexuality; it is a liberal leap across the tasks and struggles of here and now, the continuing process of sexual definition which will generate its own possibilities and choices. (It also assumes that women who have chosen women have done so simply because men are oppressive and emotionally unavailable, which still fails to account for women who continue to pursue relationships with oppressive and/or emotionally unsatisfying men.) I am suggesting that heterosexuality, like motherhood, needs to be recognized and studied as a *political institution*—even, or especially, by those individuals who feel they are, in their personal experience, the precursors of a new social relation between the sexes.

II

If women are the earliest sources of emotional caring and physical nurture for both female and male children, it would seem logical, from a feminist perspective at least, to pose the following questions: whether the search for love and tenderness in both sexes does not originally lead toward women; *why in fact women would ever redirect that search;* why species survival, the means of impregnation, and emotional/erotic relationships should ever have become so rigidly identified with each other; and why such violent strictures should be found necessary to enforce women's total emotional, erotic loyalty and subservience to men. I doubt that enough feminist scholars and theorists have taken the pains to acknowledge the societal forces which wrench women's emotional and erotic energies away from themselves and other women and from woman-identified values. These forces, as I shall try to show, range from literal physical enslavement to the disguising and distorting of possible options.

I do not assume that mothering by women is a "sufficient

cause" of lesbian existence. But the issue of mothering by women has been much in the air of late, usually accompanied by the view that increased parenting by men would minimize antagonism between the sexes and equalize the sexual imbalance of power of males over females. These discussions are carried on without reference to compulsory heterosexuality as a phenomenon, let alone as an ideology. I do not wish to psychologize here, but rather to identify sources of male power. I believe large numbers of men could, in fact, undertake child care on a large scale without radically altering the balance of male power in a male-identified society.

In her essay "The Origin of the Family," Kathleen Gough lists eight characteristics of male power in archaic and contemporary societies which I would like to use as a framework: "men's ability to deny women sexuality or to force it upon them; to command or exploit their labor to control their produce; to control or rob them of their children; to confine them physically and prevent their movement; to use them as objects in male transactions; to cramp their creativeness; or to withhold from them large areas of the society's knowledge and cultural attainments."[14] (Gough does not perceive these power characteristics as specifically enforcing heterosexuality, only as producing sexual inequality.) Below, Gough's words appear in italics; the elaboration of each of her categories, in brackets, is my own.

Characteristics of male power include *the power of men*

1. *to deny women* [their own] *sexuality*—[by means of clitoridectomy and infibulation; chastity belts; punishment, including death, for female adultery; punishment, including death, for

14. Kathleen Gough, "The Origin of the Family," in *Toward an Anthropology of Women*, ed. Rayna [Rapp] Reiter (New York: Monthly Review Press, 1975), pp. 69–70.

lesbian sexuality; psychoanalytic denial of the clitoris; strictures
against masturbation; denial of maternal and postmenopausal
sensuality; unnecessary hysterectomy; pseudolesbian images in
the media and literature; closing of archives and destruction of
documents relating to lesbian existence]

2. *or to force it* [male sexuality] *upon them*—[by means of rape
(including marital rape) and wife beating; father-daughter,
brother-sister incest; the socialization of women to feel that
male sexual "drive" amounts to a right;[15] idealization of hetero-
sexual romance in art, literature, the media, advertising, etc.;
child marriage; arranged marriage; prostitution; the harem; psy-
choanalytic doctrines of frigidity and vaginal orgasm; porno-
graphic depictions of women responding pleasurably to sexual
violence and humiliation (a subliminal message being that sadis-
tic heterosexuality is more "normal" than sensuality between
women)]

3. *to command or exploit their labor to control their produce*—[by
means of the institutions of marriage and motherhood as unpaid
production; the horizontal segregation of women in paid em-
ployment; the decoy of the upwardly mobile token woman;
male control of abortion, contraception, sterilization, and child-
birth; pimping; female infanticide, which robs mothers of
daughters and contributes to generalized devaluation of
women]

4. *to control or rob them of their children*—[by means of father
right and "legal kidnaping";[16] enforced sterilization; systema-
tized infanticide; seizure of children from lesbian mothers by
the courts; the malpractice of male obstetrics; use of the mother
as "token torturer"[17] in genital mutilation or in binding the
daughter's feet (or mind) to fit her for marriage]

5. *to confine them physically and prevent their movement*—[by
means of rape as terrorism, keeping women off the streets;
purdah; foot binding; atrophying of women's athletic capabili-
ties; high heels and "feminine" dress codes in fashion; the veil;
sexual harassment on the streets; horizontal segregation of

---

15. Barry, pp. 216–219.
16. Anna Demeter, *Legal Kidnapping* (Boston: Beacon, 1977), pp. xx, 126–128.
17. Daly, pp. 139–141, 163–165.

women in employment; prescriptions for "full-time" mothering at home; enforced economic dependence of wives]

6. *to use them as objects in male transactions*—[use of women as "gifts"; bride price; pimping; arranged marriage; use of women as entertainers to facilitate male deals—e.g., wife-hostess, cocktail waitress required to dress for male sexual titillation, call girls, "bunnies," geisha, *kisaeng* prostitutes, secretaries]

7. *to cramp their creativeness*—[witch persecutions as campaigns against midwives and female healers, and as pogrom against independent, "unassimilated" women;[18] definition of male pursuits as more valuable than female within any culture, so that cultural values become the embodiment of male subjectivity; restriction of female self-fulfillment to marriage and motherhood; sexual exploitation of women by male artists and teachers; the social and economic disruption of women's creative aspirations;[19] erasure of female tradition][20]

8. *to withhold from them large areas of the society's knowledge and cultural attainments*—[by means of noneducation of females; the "Great Silence" regarding women and particularly lesbian existence in history and culture;[21] sex-role tracking which deflects women from science, technology, and other "masculine" pursuits; male social/professional bonding which excludes women; discrimination against women in the professions]

These are some of the methods by which male power is manifested and maintained. Looking at the schema, what surely impresses itself is the fact that we are confronting not a simple maintenance of inequality and property possession,

18. Barbara Ehrenreich and Deirdre English, *Witches, Midwives and Nurses: A History of Women Healers* (Old Westbury, N.Y.: Feminist Press, 1973); Andrea Dworkin, *Woman Hating* (New York: Dutton, 1974), pp. 118–154; Daly, pp. 178–222.

19. See Virginia Woolf, *A Room of One's Own* (London: Hogarth, 1929), and *id.*, *Three Guineas* (New York: Harcourt Brace, [1938] 1966); Tillie Olsen, *Silences* (Boston: Delacorte, 1978); Michelle Cliff, "The Resonance of Interruption," *Chrysalis: A Magazine of Women's Culture* 8 (1979): 29–37.

20. Mary Daly, *Beyond God the Father* (Boston: Beacon, 1973), pp. 347–351; Olsen, pp. 22–46.

21. Daly, *Beyond God the Father*, p. 93.

but a pervasive cluster of forces, ranging from physical brutality to control of consciousness, which suggests that an enormous potential counterforce is having to be restrained.

Some of the forms by which male power manifests itself are more easily recognizable as enforcing heterosexuality on women than are others. Yet each one I have listed adds to the cluster of forces within which women have been convinced that marriage and sexual orientation toward men are inevitable —even if unsatisfying or oppressive—components of their lives. The chastity belt; child marriage; erasure of lesbian existence (except as exotic and perverse) in art, literature, film; idealization of heterosexual romance and marriage—these are some fairly obvious forms of compulsion, the first two exemplifying physical force, the second two control of consciousness. While clitoridectomy has been assailed by feminists as a form of woman torture,[22] Kathleen Barry first pointed out that it is not simply a way of turning the young girl into a "marriageable" woman through brutal surgery. It intends that women in the intimate proximity of polygynous marriage will not form sexual relationships with each other, that—from a male, genital-fetishist perspective—female erotic connections, even in a sex-segregated situation, will be literally excised.[23]

The function of pornography as an influence on consciousness is a major public issue of our time, when a multibillion-dollar industry has the power to disseminate increasingly sadistic, women-degrading visual images. But even so-called soft-core pornography and advertising depict women as objects of sexual appetite devoid of emotional context, without individ-

22. Fran P. Hosken, "The Violence of Power: Genital Mutilation of Females," *Heresies: A Feminist Journal of Art and Politics* 6 (1979): 28–35; Russell and van de Ven, pp. 194–195.

[A.R., 1986: See especially "Circumcision of Girls," in Nawal El Saadawi, *The Hidden Face of Eve: Women in the Arab World* (Boston: Beacon, 1982), pp. 33–43.]

23. Barry, pp. 163–164.

ual meaning or personality—essentially as a sexual commodity to be consumed by males. (So-called lesbian pornography, created for the male voyeuristic eye, is equally devoid of emotional context or individual personality.) The most pernicious message relayed by pornography is that women are natural sexual prey to men and love it, that sexuality and violence are congruent, and that for women sex is essentially masochistic, humiliation pleasurable, physical abuse erotic. But along with this message comes another, not always recognized: that enforced submission and the use of cruelty, if played out in heterosexual pairing, is sexually "normal," while sensuality between women, including erotic mutuality and respect, is "queer," "sick," and either pornographic in itself or not very exciting compared with the sexuality of whips and bondage.[24] Pornography does not simply create a climate in which sex and violence are interchangeable; *it widens the range of behavior considered acceptable from men in heterosexual intercourse*— behavior which reiteratively strips women of their autonomy, dignity, and sexual potential, including the potential of loving and being loved by women in mutuality and integrity.

In her brilliant study *Sexual Harassment of Working Women: A Case of Sex Discrimination*, Catharine A. MacKinnon delineates the intersection of compulsory heterosexuality and economics. Under capitalism, women are horizontally segregated by gender and occupy a structurally inferior position in the workplace. This is hardly news, but MacKinnon raises the question why, even if capitalism "requires some collection of individuals to occupy low-status, low-paying positions . . . such persons must be biologically female," and goes on to point out that "the fact that male employers often do not hire qua-

24. The issue of "lesbian sadomasochism" needs to be examined in terms of dominant cultures' teachings about the relation of sex and violence. I believe this to be another example of the "double life" of women.

lified women, *even when they could pay them less than men* suggests that more than the profit motive is implicated" [emphasis added].[25] She cites a wealth of material documenting the fact that women are not only segregated in low-paying service jobs (as secretaries, domestics, nurses, typists, telephone operators, child-care workers, waitresses), but that "sexualization of the woman" is part of the job. Central and intrinsic to the economic realities of women's lives is the requirement that women will "market sexual attractiveness to men, who tend to hold the economic power and position to enforce their predilections." And MacKinnon documents that "sexual harassment perpetuates the interlocked structure by which women have been kept sexually in thrall to men at the bottom of the labor market. Two forces of American society converge: men's control over women's sexuality and capital's control over employees' work lives."[26] Thus, women in the workplace are at the mercy of sex as power in a vicious circle. Economically disadvantaged, women—whether waitresses or professors—endure sexual harassment to keep their jobs and learn to behave in a complaisantly and ingratiatingly heterosexual manner because they discover this is their true qualification for employment, whatever the job description. And, MacKinnon notes, the woman who too decisively resists sexual overtures in the workplace is accused of being "dried up" and sexless, or lesbian. This raises a specific difference between the experiences of lesbians and homosexual men. A lesbian, closeted on her job because of heterosexist prejudice, is not simply forced into denying the truth of her outside relationships or private life. Her job depends on her pretending to be not merely heterosexual, but a heterosexual *woman* in terms of dressing and playing

25. Catharine A. MacKinnon, *Sexual Harassment of Working Women: A Case of Sex Discrimination* (New Haven, Conn.: Yale University Press, 1979), pp. 15–16.
26. *Ibid.*, p. 174.

the feminine, deferential role required of "real" women.

MacKinnon raises radical questions as to the qualitative differences between sexual harassment, rape, and ordinary heterosexual intercourse. ("As one accused rapist put it, he hadn't used 'any more force than is usual for males during the preliminaries.' ") She criticizes Susan Brownmiller[27] for separating rape from the mainstream of daily life and for her unexamined premise that "rape is violence, intercourse is sexuality," removing rape from the sexual sphere altogether. Most crucially she argues that "taking rape from the realm of 'the sexual,' placing it in the realm of 'the violent,' allows one to be against it without raising any questions about the extent to which the institution of heterosexuality has defined force as a normal part of 'the preliminaries.' "[28] "Never is it asked whether, under conditions of male supremacy, the notion of 'consent' has any meaning."[29]

The fact is that the workplace, among other social institutions, is a place where women have learned to accept male violation of their psychic and physical boundaries as the price of survival; where women have been educated—no less than by romantic literature or by pornography—to perceive themselves as sexual prey. A woman seeking to escape such casual violations along with economic disadvantage may well turn to marriage as a form of hoped-for protection, while bringing into marriage neither social nor economic power, thus entering that institution also from a disadvantaged position. MacKinnon finally asks:

27. Brownmiller, *op. cit.*

28. MacKinnon, p. 219. Susan Schecter writes: "The push for heterosexual union at whatever cost is so intense that . . . it has become a cultural force of its own that creates battering. The ideology of romantic love and its jealous possession of the partner as property provide the masquerade for what can become severe abuse" (*Aegis: Magazine on Ending Violence against Women* [July–August 1979]: 50–51).

29. MacKinnon, p. 298.

What if inequality is built into the social conceptions of male and female sexuality, of masculinity and femininity, of sexiness and heterosexual attractiveness? Incidents of sexual harassment suggest that male sexual desire itself may be aroused by female vulnerability. . . . Men feel they can take advantage, so they want to, so they do. Examination of sexual harassment, precisely because the episodes appear commonplace, forces one to confront the fact that sexual intercourse normally occurs between economic (as well as physical) unequals . . . the apparent legal requirement that violations of women's sexuality appear out of the ordinary before they will be punished helps prevent women from defining the ordinary conditions of their own consent.[30]

Given the nature and extent of heterosexual pressures—the daily "eroticization of women's subordination," as MacKinnon phrases it[31]—I question the more or less psychoanalytic perspective (suggested by such writers as Karen Horney, H. R. Hayes, Wolfgang Lederer, and, most recently, Dorothy Dinnerstein) that the male need to control women sexually results from some primal male "fear of women" and of women's sexual insatiability. It seems more probable that men really fear not that they will have women's sexual appetites forced on them or that women want to smother and devour them, but that women could be indifferent to them altogether, that men could be allowed sexual and emotional—therefore economic—access to women *only* on women's terms, otherwise being left on the periphery of the matrix.

The means of assuring male sexual access to women have recently received searching investigation by Kathleen Barry.[32] She documents extensive and appalling evidence for the exis-

30. *Ibid.*, p. 220.
31. *Ibid.*, p. 221.
32. Barry, *op. cit.*
[A.R., 1986: See also Kathleen Barry, Charlotte Bunch, and Shirley Castley, eds., *International Feminism: Networking against Female Sexual Slavery* (New York: International Women's Tribune Center, 1984).]

tence, on a very large scale, of international female slavery, the institution once known as "white slavery" but which in fact has involved, and at this very moment involves, women of every race and class. In the theoretical analysis derived from her research, Barry makes the connection between all enforced conditions under which women live subject to men: prostitution, marital rape, father-daughter and brother-sister incest, wife beating, pornography, bride price, the selling of daughters, purdah, and genital mutilation. She sees the rape paradigm—where the victim of sexual assault is held responsible for her own victimization—as leading to the rationalization and acceptance of other forms of enslavement where the woman is presumed to have "chosen" her fate, to embrace it passively, or to have courted it perversely through rash or unchaste behavior. On the contrary, Barry maintains, "female sexual slavery is present in ALL situations where women or girls cannot change the conditions of their existence; where regardless of how they got into those conditions, e.g., social pressure, economic hardship, misplaced trust or the longing for affection, they cannot get out; and where they are subject to sexual violence and exploitation."[33] She provides a spectrum of concrete examples, not only as to the existence of a widespread international traffic in women, but also as to how this operates—whether in the form of a "Minnesota pipeline" funneling blonde, blue-eyed midwestern runaways to Times Square, or the purchasing of young women out of rural poverty in Latin America or Southeast Asia, or the providing of *maisons d'abattage* for migrant workers in the eighteenth arrondissement of Paris. Instead of "blaming the victim" or trying to diagnose her presumed pathology, Barry turns her floodlight on the pathology of sex colonization itself, the ide-

33. Barry, p. 33.

ology of "cultural sadism" represented by the pornography industry and by the overall identification of women primarily as "sexual beings whose responsibility is the sexual service of men."[34]

Barry delineates what she names a "sexual domination perspective" through whose lens sexual abuse and terrorism of women by men has been rendered almost invisible by treating it as natural and inevitable. From its point of view, women are expendable as long as the sexual and emotional needs of the male can be satisfied. To replace this perspective of domination with a universal standard of basic freedom for women from gender-specific violence, from constraints on movement, and from male right of sexual and emotional access is the political purpose of her book. Like Mary Daly in *Gyn/Ecology*, Barry rejects structuralist and other cultural-relativist rationalizations for sexual torture and anti-woman violence. In her opening chapter, she asks of her readers that they refuse all handy escapes into ignorance and denial. "The only way we can come out of hiding, break through our paralyzing defenses, is to know it all—the full extent of sexual violence and domination of women. . . . In *knowing*, in facing directly, we can learn to chart our course out of this oppression, by envisioning and creating a world which will preclude sexual slavery."[35]

"Until we name the practice, give conceptual definition and form to it, illustrate its life over time and in space, those who are its most obvious victims will also not be able to name it or define their experience."

But women are all, in different ways and to different degrees, its victims; and part of the problem with naming and conceptu-

34. *Ibid.*, p. 103.
35. *Ibid.*, p. 5.

alizing female sexual slavery is, as Barry clearly sees, compulsory heterosexuality.[36] Compulsory heterosexuality simplifies the task of the procurer and pimp in world-wide prostitution rings and "eros centers," while, in the privacy of the home, it leads the daughter to "accept" incest/rape by her father, the mother to deny that it is happening, the battered wife to stay on with an abusive husband. "Befriending or love" is a major tactic of the procurer, whose job it is to turn the runaway or the confused young girl over to the pimp for seasoning. The ideology of heterosexual romance, beamed at her from childhood out of fairy tales, television, films, advertising, popular songs, wedding pageantry, is a tool ready to the procurer's hand and one which he does not hesitate to use, as Barry documents. Early female indoctrination in "love" as an emotion may be largely a Western concept; but a more universal ideology concerns the primacy and uncontrollability of the male sexual drive. This is one of many insights offered by Barry's work:

> As sexual power is learned by adolescent boys through the social experience of their sex drive, so do girls learn that the locus of sexual power is male. Given the importance placed on the male sex drive in the socialization of girls as well as boys, early adolescence is probably the first significant phase of male identification in a girl's life and development. . . . As a young girl becomes aware of her own increasing sexual feelings . . . she turns away from her heretofore primary relationships with girlfriends. As they become secondary to her, recede in importance in her life, her own identity also assumes a secondary role and she grows into male identification.[37]

36. *Ibid.*, p. 100.

[A.R., 1986: This statement has been taken as claiming that "all women are victims" purely and simply, or that "all heterosexuality equals sexual slavery." I would say, rather, that all women are affected, though differently, by dehumanizing attitudes and practices directed at women as a group.]

37. *Ibid.*, p. 218.

We still need to ask why some women never, even temporarily, turn away from "heretofore primary relationships" with other females. And why does male identification—the casting of one's social, political, and intellectual allegiances with men —exist among lifelong sexual lesbians? Barry's hypothesis throws us among new questions, but it clarifies the diversity of forms in which compulsory heterosexuality presents itself. In the mystique of the overpowering, all-conquering male sex drive, the penis-with-a-life-of-its own, is rooted the law of male sex right to women, which justifies prostitution as a universal cultural assumption on the one hand, while defending sexual slavery within the family on the basis of "family privacy and cultural uniqueness" on the other.[38] The adolescent male sex drive, which, as both young women and men are taught, once triggered cannot take responsibility for itself or take no for an answer, becomes, according to Barry, the norm and rationale for adult male sexual behavior: a condition of *arrested sexual development.* Women learn to accept as natural the inevitability of this "drive" because they receive it as dogma. Hence, marital rape; hence, the Japanese wife resignedly packing her husband's suitcase for a weekend in the *kisaeng* brothels of Taiwan; hence, the psychological as well as economic imbalance of power between husband and wife, male employer and female worker, father and daughter, male professor and female student. The effect of male identification means

internalizing the values of the colonizer and actively participating in carrying out the colonization of one's self and one's sex. . . . Male identification is the act whereby women place men above women, including themselves, in credibility, status, and importance in most situations, regardless of the comparative quality the women

38. *Ibid.*, p. 140.

may bring to the situation. . . . Interaction with women is seen as
a lesser form of relating on every level.[39]

What deserves further exploration is the doublethink many
women engage in and from which no woman is permanently
and utterly free: However woman-to-woman relationships, fe-
male support networks, a female and feminist value system are
relied on and cherished, indoctrination in male credibility and
status can still create synapses in thought, denials of feeling,
wishful thinking, a profound sexual and intellectual confu-
sion.[40] I quote here from a letter I received the day I was
writing this passage: "I have had very bad relationships with
men—I am now in the midst of a very painful separation. I am
trying to find my strength through women—without my
friends, I could not survive." How many times a day do women
speak words like these or think them or write them, and how
often does the synapse reassert itself?

Barry summarizes her findings:

Considering the arrested sexual development that is understood to
be normal in the male population, and considering the numbers
of men who are pimps, procurers, members of slavery gangs, cor-
rupt officials participating in this traffic, owners, operators, em-
ployees of brothels and lodging and entertainment facilities, por-
nography purveyors, associated with prostitution, wife beaters,
child molesters, incest perpetrators, johns (tricks) and rapists, one
cannot but be momentarily stunned by the enormous male popula-
tion engaging in female sexual slavery. The huge number of men
engaged in these practices should be cause for declaration of an

39. *Ibid.*, p. 172.
40. Elsewhere I have suggested that male identification has been a powerful source
of white women's racism and that it has often been women already seen as "disloyal"
to male codes and systems who have actively battled against it (Adrienne Rich,
"Disloyal to Civilization: Feminism, Racism, Gynephobia," in *On Lies, Secrets, and
Silence: Selected Prose, 1966–1978* [New York: W. W. Norton, 1979]).

international emergency, a crisis in sexual violence. But what should be cause for alarm is instead accepted as normal sexual intercourse.[41]

Susan Cavin, in a rich and provocative, if highly speculative, dissertation, suggests that patriarchy becomes possible when the original female band, which includes children but ejects adolescent males, becomes invaded and outnumbered by males; that not patriarchal marriage, but the rape of the mother by the son, becomes the first act of male domination. The entering wedge, or leverage, which allows this to happen is not just a simple change in sex ratios; it is also the mother-child bond, manipulated by adolescent males in order to remain within the matrix past the age of exclusion. Maternal affection is used to establish male right of sexual access, which, however, must ever after be held by force (or through control of consciousness) since the original deep adult bonding is that of woman for woman.[42] I find this hypothesis extremely suggestive, since one form of false consciousness which serves compulsory heterosexuality is the maintenance of a mother-son relationship between women and men, including the demand that women provide maternal solace, nonjudgmental nurturing, and compassion for their harassers, rapists, and batterers (as well as for men who passively vampirize them).

But whatever its origins, when we look hard and clearly at the extent and elaboration of measures designed to keep women within a male sexual purlieu, it becomes an inescapable question whether the issue feminists have to address is not simple "gender inequality" nor the domination of culture by

41. Barry, p. 220.
42. Susan Cavin, "Lesbian Origins" (Ph.D. diss., Rutgers University, 1978), unpublished, ch. 6.
[A.R., 1986: This dissertation was recently published as *Lesbian Origins* (San Francisco: Ism Press, 1986).]

males nor mere "taboos against homosexuality," but the en-
forcement of heterosexuality for women as a means of assuring
male right of physical, economic, and emotional access.[43] One
of many means of enforcement is, of course, the rendering
invisible of the lesbian possibility, an engulfed continent which
rises fragmentedly into view from time to time only to become
submerged again. Feminist research and theory that contribute
to lesbian invisibility or marginality are actually working
against the liberation and empowerment of women as a
group.[44]

The assumption that "most women are innately heterosex-
ual" stands as a theoretical and political stumbling block for
feminism. It remains a tenable assumption partly because les-
bian existence has been written out of history or catalogued
under disease, partly because it has been treated as exceptional
rather than intrinsic, partly because to acknowledge that for
women heterosexuality may not be a "preference" at all but
something that has had to be imposed, managed, organized,
propagandized, and maintained by force is an immense step to
take if you consider yourself freely and "innately" heterosexual.

43. For my perception of heterosexuality as an economic institution I am indebted
to Lisa Leghorn and Katherine Parker, who allowed me to read the unpublished
manuscript of their book *Woman's Worth: Sexual Economics and the World of
Women* (London and Boston: Routledge & Kegan Paul, 1981).

44. I would suggest that lesbian existence has been most recognized and tolerated
where it has resembled a "deviant" version of heterosexuality—e.g., where lesbians
have, like Stein and Toklas, played heterosexual roles (or seemed to in public) and have
been chiefly identified with male culture. See also Claude E. Schaeffer, "The Kuterai
Female Berdache: Courier, Guide, Prophetess and Warrior," *Ethnohistory* 12, no. 3
(Summer 1965): 193–236. (Berdache: "an individual of a definite physiological sex [m.
or f.] who assumes the role and status of the opposite sex and who is viewed by the
community as being of one sex physiologically but as having assumed the role and
status of the opposite sex" [Schaeffer, p. 231].) Lesbian existence has also been
relegated to an upper-class phenomenon, an elite decadence (as in the fascination with
Paris salon lesbians such as Renée Vivien and Natalie Clifford Barney), to the obscur-
ing of such "common women" as Judy Grahn depicts in her *The Work of a Common
Woman* (Oakland, Calif.: Diana Press, 1978) and *True to Life Adventure Stories*
(Oakland, Calif.: Diana Press, 1978).

Yet the failure to examine heterosexuality as an institution is like failing to admit that the economic system called capitalism or the caste system of racism is maintained by a variety of forces, including both physical violence and false consciousness. To take the step of questioning heterosexuality as a "preference" or "choice" for women—and to do the intellectual and emotional work that follows—will call for a special quality of courage in heterosexually identified feminists, but I think the rewards will be great: a freeing-up of thinking, the exploring of new paths, the shattering of another great silence, new clarity in personal relationships.

III

I have chosen to use the terms *lesbian existence* and *lesbian continuum* because the word *lesbianism* has a clinical and limiting ring. *Lesbian existence* suggests both the fact of the historical presence of lesbians and our continuing creation of the meaning of that existence. I mean the term *lesbian continuum* to include a range—through each woman's life and throughout history—of woman-identified experience, not simply the fact that a woman has had or consciously desired genital sexual experience with another woman. If we expand it to embrace many more forms of primary intensity between and among women, including the sharing of a rich inner life, the bonding against male tyranny, the giving and receiving of practical and political support, if we can also hear it in such associations as *marriage resistance* and the "haggard" behavior identified by Mary Daly (obsolete meanings: "intractable," "willful," "wanton," and "unchaste," "a woman reluctant to yield to wooing"),[45] we begin to grasp breadths of female

45. Daly, *Gyn/Ecology*, p. 15.

history and psychology which have lain out of reach as a consequence of limited, mostly clinical, definitions of *lesbianism.*

Lesbian existence comprises both the breaking of a taboo and the rejection of a compulsory way of life. It is also a direct or indirect attack on male right of access to women. But it is more than these, although we may first begin to perceive it as a form of naysaying to patriarchy, an act of resistance. It has, of course, included isolation, self-hatred, breakdown, alcoholism, suicide, and intrawoman violence; we romanticize at our peril what it means to love and act against the grain, and under heavy penalties; and lesbian existence has been lived (unlike, say, Jewish or Catholic existence) without access to any knowledge of a tradition, a continuity, a social underpinning. The destruction of records and memorabilia and letters documenting the realities of lesbian existence must be taken very seriously as a means of keeping heterosexuality compulsory for women, since what has been kept from our knowledge is joy, sensuality, courage, and community, as well as guilt, self-betrayal, and pain.[46]

Lesbians have historically been deprived of a political existence through "inclusion" as female versions of male homosexuality. To equate lesbian existence with male homosexuality because each is stigmatized is to erase female reality once again. Part of the history of lesbian existence is, obviously, to be found where lesbians, lacking a coherent female commu-

---

46. "In a hostile world in which women are not supposed to survive except in relation with and in service to men, entire communities of women were simply erased. History tends to bury what it seeks to reject" (Blanche W. Cook, " 'Women Alone Stir My Imagination': Lesbianism and the Cultural Tradition," *Signs: Journal of Women in Culture and Society* 4, no. 4 [Summer 1979]: 719–720). The Lesbian Herstory Archives in New York City is one attempt to preserve contemporary documents on lesbian existence—a project of enormous value and meaning, working against the continuing censorship and obliteration of relationships, networks, communities in other archives and elsewhere in the culture.

nity, have shared a kind of social life and common cause with homosexual men. But there are differences: women's lack of economic and cultural privilege relative to men; qualitative differences in female and male relationships—for example, the patterns of anonymous sex among male homosexuals, and the pronounced ageism in male homosexual standards of sexual attractiveness. I perceive the lesbian experience as being, like motherhood, a profoundly *female* experience, with particular oppressions, meanings, and potentialities we cannot comprehend as long as we simply bracket it with other sexually stigmatized existences. Just as the term *parenting* serves to conceal the particular and significant reality of being a parent who is actually a mother, the term *gay* may serve the purpose of blurring the very outlines we need to discern, which are of crucial value for feminism and for the freedom of women as a group.[47]

As the term *lesbian* has been held to limiting, clinical associations in its patriarchal definition, female friendship and comradeship have been set apart from the erotic, thus limiting the erotic itself. But as we deepen and broaden the range of what we define as lesbian existence, as we delineate a lesbian continuum, we begin to discover the erotic in female terms: as that which is unconfined to any single part of the body or solely to the body itself; as an energy not only diffuse but, as Audre Lorde has described it, omnipresent in "the sharing of joy, whether physical, emotional, psychic," and in the sharing of work; as the empowering joy which "makes us less willing to accept powerlessness, or those other supplied states of being which are not native to me, such as resignation, despair, self-

47. [A.R., 1986: The shared historical and spiritual "crossover" functions of lesbians and gay men in cultures past and present are traced by Judy Grahn in *Another Mother Tongue: Gay Words, Gay Worlds* (Boston: Beacon, 1984). I now think we have much to learn both from the uniquely female aspects of lesbian existence and from the complex "gay" identity we share with gay men.]

effacement, depression, self-denial."[48] In another context, writing of women and work, I quoted the autobiographical passage in which the poet H.D. described how her friend Bryher supported her in persisting with the visionary experience which was to shape her mature work:

> I knew that this experience, this writing-on-the-wall before me, could not be shared with anyone except the girl who stood so bravely there beside me. This girl said without hesitation, "Go on." It was she really who had the detachment and integrity of the Pythoness of Delphi. But it was I, battered and dissociated . . . who was seeing the pictures, and who was reading the writing or granted the inner vision. Or perhaps, in some sense, we were "seeing" it together, for without her, admittedly, I could not have gone on.[49]

If we consider the possibility that all women—from the infant suckling at her mother's breast, to the grown woman experiencing orgasmic sensations while suckling her own child, perhaps recalling her mother's milk smell in her own, to two women, like Virginia Woolf's Chloe and Olivia, who share a laboratory,[50] to the woman dying at ninety, touched and handled by women—exist on a lesbian continuum, we can see ourselves as moving in and out of this continuum, whether we identify ourselves as lesbian or not.

We can then connect aspects of woman identification as diverse as the impudent, intimate girl friendships of eight or nine year olds and the banding together of those women of the twelfth and fifteenth centuries known as Beguines who "shared

48. Audre Lorde, "Uses of the Erotic: The Erotic as Power," in *Sister Outsider* (Trumansburg, N.Y.: Crossing Press, 1984).

49. Adrienne Rich, "Conditions for Work: The Common World of Women," in *On Lies, Secrets, and Silence,* p. 209; H.D., *Tribute to Freud* (Oxford: Carcanet, 1971), pp. 50–54.

50. Woolf, *A Room of One's Own,* p. 126.

houses, rented to one another, bequeathed houses to their room-mates . . . in cheap subdivided houses in the artisans' area of town," who "practiced Christian virtue on their own, dressing and living simply and not associating with men," who earned their livings as spinsters, bakers, nurses, or ran schools for young girls, and who managed—until the Church forced them to disperse—to live independent both of marriage and of conventual restrictions.[51] It allows us to connect these women with the more celebrated "Lesbians" of the women's school around Sappho of the seventh century B.C., with the secret sororities and economic networks reported among African women, and with the Chinese marriage-resistance sisterhoods —communities of women who refused marriage or who, if married, often refused to consummate their marriages and soon left their husbands, the only women in China who were not footbound and who, Agnes Smedley tells us, welcomed the births of daughters and organized successful women's strikes in the silk mills.[52] It allows us to connect and compare disparate individual instances of marriage resistance: for example, the strategies available to Emily Dickinson, a nineteenth-century white woman genius, with the strategies available to Zora Neale Hurston, a twentieth-century Black woman genius. Dickinson never married, had tenuous intellectual friendships with

51. Gracia Clark, "The Beguines: A Mediaeval Women's Community," *Quest: A Feminist Quarterly* 1, no. 4 (1975): 73–80.
52. See Denise Paulmé, ed., *Women of Tropical Africa* (Berkeley: University of California Press, 1963), pp. 7, 266–267. Some of these sororities are described as "a kind of defensive syndicate against the male element," their aims being "to offer concerted resistance to an oppressive patriarchate," "independence in relation to one's husband and with regard to motherhood, mutual aid, satisfaction of personal revenge." See also Audre Lorde, "Scratching the Surface: Some Notes on Barriers to Women and Loving," in *Sister Outsider*, pp. 45–52; Marjorie Topley, "Marriage Resistance in Rural Kwangtung," in *Women in Chinese Society*, ed. M. Wolf and R. Witke (Stanford, Calif.: Stanford University Press, 1978), pp. 67–89; Agnes Smedley, *Portraits of Chinese Women in Revolution*, ed. J. MacKinnon and S. MacKinnon (Old Westbury, N.Y.: Feminist Press, 1976), pp. 103–110.

men, lived self-convented in her genteel father's house in Am-
herst, and wrote a lifetime of passionate letters to her sister-in-
law Sue Gilbert and a smaller group of such letters to her friend
Kate Scott Anthon. Hurston married twice but soon left each
husband, scrambled her way from Florida to Harlem to Co-
lumbia University to Haiti and finally back to Florida, moved
in and out of white patronage and poverty, professional success,
and failure; her survival relationships were all with women,
beginning with her mother. Both of these women in their
vastly different circumstances were marriage resisters, commit-
ted to their own work and selfhood, and were later character-
ized as "apolitical." Both were drawn to men of intellectual
quality; for both of them women provided the ongoing fascina-
tion and sustenance of life.

If we think of heterosexuality as *the* natural emotional and
sensual inclination for women, lives such as these are seen as
deviant, as pathological, or as emotionally and sensually de-
prived. Or, in more recent and permissive jargon, they are
banalized as "life styles." And the work of such women,
whether merely the daily work of individual or collective sur-
vival and resistance or the work of the writer, the activist, the
reformer, the anthropologist, or the artist—the work of self-
creation—is undervalued, or seen as the bitter fruit of "penis
envy" or the sublimation of repressed eroticism or the mean-
ingless rant of a "man-hater." But when we turn the lens of
vision and consider the degree to which and the methods
whereby heterosexual "preference" has actually been imposed
on women, not only can we understand differently the meaning
of individual lives and work, but we can begin to recognize a
central fact of women's history: that women have always re-
sisted male tyranny. A feminism of action, often though not
always without a theory, has constantly re-emerged in every
culture and in every period. We can then begin to study

women's struggle against powerlessness, women's radical rebellion, not just in male-defined "concrete revolutionary situations"[53] but in all the situations male ideologies have not perceived as revolutionary—for example, the refusal of some women to produce children, aided at great risk by other women;[54] the refusal to produce a higher standard of living and leisure for men (Leghorn and Parker show how both are part of women's unacknowledged, unpaid, and ununionized economic contribution). We can no longer have patience with Dinnerstein's view that women have simply collaborated with men in the "sexual arrangements" of history. We begin to observe behavior, both in history and in individual biography, that has hitherto been invisible or misnamed, behavior which often constitutes, given the limits of the counterforce exerted in a given time and place, radical rebellion. And we can connect these rebellions and the necessity for them with the physical passion of woman for woman which is central to lesbian existence: the erotic sensuality which has been, precisely, the most violently erased fact of female experience.

Heterosexuality has been both forcibly and subliminally imposed on women. Yet everywhere women have resisted it, often at the cost of physical torture, imprisonment, psychosurgery, social ostracism, and extreme poverty. "Compulsory heterosexuality" was named as one of the "crimes against women" by the Brussels International Tribunal on Crimes against Women in 1976. Two pieces of testimony from two very different cultures reflect the degree to which persecution of

53. See Rosalind Petchesky, "Dissolving the Hyphen: A Report on Marxist-Feminist Groups 1–5," in *Capitalist Patriarchy and the Case for Socialist Feminism*, ed. Zillah Eisenstein (New York: Monthly Review Press, 1979), p. 387.

54. [A.R., 1986: See Angela Davis, *Women, Race and Class* (New York: Random House, 1981), p. 102; Orlando Patterson, *Slavery and Social Death: A Comparative Study* (Cambridge: Harvard University Press, 1982), p. 133.]

lesbians is a global practice here and now. A report from Norway relates:

> A lesbian in Oslo was in a heterosexual marriage that didn't work, so she started taking tranquillizers and ended up at the health sanatorium for treatment and rehabilitation. . . . The moment she said in family group therapy that she believed she was a lesbian, the doctor told her she was not. He knew from "looking into her eyes," he said. She had the eyes of a woman who wanted sexual intercourse with her husband. So she was subjected to so-called "couch therapy." She was put into a comfortably heated room, naked, on a bed, and for an hour her husband was to . . . try to excite her sexually. . . . The idea was that the touching was always to end with sexual intercourse. She felt stronger and stronger aversion. She threw up and sometimes ran out of the room to avoid this "treatment." The more strongly she asserted that she was a lesbian, the more violent the forced heterosexual intercourse became. This treatment went on for about six months. She escaped from the hospital, but she was brought back. Again she escaped. She has not been there since. In the end she realized that she had been subjected to forcible rape for six months.

And from Mozambique:

> I am condemned to a life of exile because I will not deny that I am a lesbian, that my primary commitments are, and will always be to other women. In the new Mozambique, lesbianism is considered a left-over from colonialism and decadent Western civilization. Lesbians are sent to rehabilitation camps to learn through self-criticism the correct line about themselves. . . . If I am forced to denounce my own love for women, if I therefore denounce myself, I could go back to Mozambique and join forces in the exciting and hard struggle of rebuilding a nation, including the struggle for the emancipation of Mozambiquan women. As it is, I either risk the rehabilitation camps, or remain in exile.[55]

55. Russell and van de Ven, pp. 42–43, 56–57.

Nor can it be assumed that women like those in Carroll Smith-Rosenberg's study, who married, stayed married, yet dwelt in a profoundly female emotional and passional world, "preferred" or "chose" heterosexuality. Women have married because it was necessary, in order to survive economically, in order to have children who would not suffer economic deprivation or social ostracism, in order to remain respectable, in order to do what was expected of women, because coming out of "abnormal" childhoods they wanted to feel "normal" and because heterosexual romance has been represented as the great female adventure, duty, and fulfillment. We may faithfully or ambivalently have obeyed the institution, but our feelings— and our sensuality—have not been tamed or contained within it. There is no statistical documentation of the numbers of lesbians who have remained in heterosexual marriages for most of their lives. But in a letter to the early lesbian publication *The Ladder*, the playwright Lorraine Hansberry had this to say:

I suspect that the problem of the married woman who would prefer emotional-physical relationships with other women is proportionally much higher than a similar statistic for men. (A statistic surely no one will ever really have.) This because the estate of woman being what it is, how could we ever begin to guess the numbers of women who are not prepared to risk a life alien to what they have been taught all their lives to believe was their "natural" destiny—AND—their only expectation for ECONOMIC security. It seems to be that this is why the question has an immensity that it does not have for male homosexuals. . . . A woman of strength and honesty may, if she chooses, sever her marriage and marry a new male mate and society will be upset that the divorce rate is rising so—but there are few places in the United States, in any event, where she will be anything remotely akin to an "outcast." Obviously this is not true for a woman who would end her marriage to take up life with another woman.[56]

This *double life*—this apparent acquiescence to an institution founded on male interest and prerogative—has been characteristic of female experience: in motherhood and in many kinds of heterosexual behavior, including the rituals of courtship; the pretense of asexuality by the nineteenth-century wife; the simulation of orgasm by the prostitute, the courtesan, the twentieth-century "sexually liberated" woman.

Meridel LeSueur's documentary novel of the depression, *The Girl,* is arresting as a study of female double life. The protagonist, a waitress in a St. Paul working-class speakeasy, feels herself passionately attracted to the young man Butch, but her survival relationships are with Clara, an older waitress and prostitute, with Belle, whose husband owns the bar, and with Amelia, a union activist. For Clara and Belle and the unnamed protagonist, sex with men is in one sense an escape from the bedrock misery of daily life, a flare of intensity in the gray, relentless, often brutal web of day-to-day existence:

> It was like he was a magnet pulling me. It was exciting and powerful and frightening. He was after me too and when he found me I would run, or be petrified, just standing in front of him like a zany. And he told me not to be wandering with Clara to the Marigold where we danced with strangers. He said he would knock

56. I am indebted to Jonathan Katz's *Gay American History (op. cit.)* for bringing to my attention Hansberry's letters to *The Ladder* and to Barbara Grier for supplying me with copies of relevant pages from *The Ladder,* quoted here by permission of Barbara Grier. See also the reprinted series of *The Ladder,* ed. Jonathan Katz et al. (New York: Arno, 1975), and Deirdre Carmody, "Letters by Eleanor Roosevelt Detail Friendship with Lorena Hickok," *New York Times* (October 21, 1979).

the shit out of me. Which made me shake and tremble, but it was better than being a husk full of suffering and not knowing why.[57]

Throughout the novel the theme of double life emerges; Belle reminisces about her marriage to the bootlegger Hoinck:

> You know, when I had that black eye and said I hit it on the cupboard, well he did it the bastard, and then he says don't tell anybody. . . . He's nuts, that's what he is, nuts, and I don't see why I live with him, why I put up with him a minute on this earth. But listen kid, she said, I'm telling you something. She looked at me and her face was wonderful. She said, Jesus Christ, Goddam him I love him that's why I'm hooked like this all my life, Goddam him I love him.[58]

After the protagonist has her first sex with Butch, her women friends care for her bleeding, give her whiskey, and compare notes.

> My luck, the first time and I got into trouble. He gave me a little money and I come to St. Paul where for ten bucks they'd stick a huge vet's needle into you and you start it and then you were on your own. . . . I never had no child. I've just had Hoinck to mother, and a hell of a child he is.[59]

> Later they made me go back to Clara's room to lie down. . . . Clara lay down beside me and put her arms around me and wanted me to tell her about it but she wanted to tell about herself. She said she started it when she was twelve with a bunch of boys in an old shed. She said nobody had paid any attention to her before and

57. Meridel LeSueur, *The Girl* (Cambridge, Mass.: West End Press, 1978), pp. 10–11. LeSueur describes, in an afterword, how this book was drawn from the writings and oral narrations of women in the Workers Alliance who met as a writers' group during the depression.
58. *Ibid.*, p. 20.
59. *Ibid.*, pp. 53–54.

she became very popular. . . . They like it so much, she said, why shouldn't you give it to them and get presents and attention? I never cared anything for it and neither did my mama. But it's the only thing you got that's valuable.[60]

Sex is thus equated with attention from the male, who is charismatic though brutal, infantile, or unreliable. Yet it is the women who make life endurable for each other, give physical affection without causing pain, share, advise, and stick by each other. *(I am trying to find my strength through women—without my friends, I could not survive.)* LeSueur's *The Girl* parallels Toni Morrison's remarkable *Sula,* another revelation of female double life:

> Nel was the one person who had wanted nothing from her, who had accepted all aspects of her. . . . Nel was one of the reasons Sula had drifted back to Medallion. . . . The men . . . had merged into one large personality: the same language of love, the same entertainments of love, the same cooling of love. Whenever she introduced her private thoughts into their rubbings and goings, they hooded their eyes. They taught her nothing but love tricks, shared nothing but worry, gave nothing but money. She had been looking all along for a friend, and it took her a while to discover that a lover was not a comrade and could never be—for a woman.

But Sula's last thought at the second of her death is "Wait'll I tell Nel." And after Sula's death, Nel looks back on her own life:

> "All that time, all that time, I thought I was missing Jude." And the loss pressed down on her chest and came up into her throat. "We was girls together," she said as though explaining something. "O Lord, Sula," she cried, "Girl, girl, girlgirlgirl!" It was a fine cry

60. *Ibid.,* p. 55.

—loud and long—but it had no bottom and it had no top, just circles and circles of sorrow.[61]

The Girl and *Sula* are both novels which examine what I am calling the lesbian continuum, in contrast to the shallow or sensational "lesbian scenes" in recent commercial fiction.[62] Each shows us woman identification untarnished (till the end of LeSueur's novel) by romanticism; each depicts the competition of heterosexual compulsion for women's attention, the diffusion and frustration of female bonding that might, in a more conscious form, reintegrate love and power.

IV

Woman identification is a source of energy, a potential springhead of female power, curtailed and contained under the institution of heterosexuality. The denial of reality and visibility to women's passion for women, women's choice of women as allies, life companions, and community, the forcing of such relationships into dissimulation and their disintegration under intense pressure have meant an incalculable loss to the power of all women *to change the social relations of the sexes, to liberate ourselves and each other.* The lie of compulsory female heterosexuality today afflicts not just feminist scholarship, but every profession, every reference work, every curriculum, every organizing attempt, every relationship or conversation over which it hovers. It creates, specifically, a profound falseness,

---

61. Toni Morrison, *Sula* (New York: Bantam, 1973), pp. 103–104, 149. I am indebted to Lorraine Bethel's essay " 'This Infinity of Conscious Pain': Zora Neale Hurston and the Black Female Literary Tradition," in *All the Women Are White, All the Blacks Are Men, but Some of Us Are Brave: Black Women's Studies,* ed. Gloria T. Hull, Patricia Bell Scott, and Barbara Smith (Old Westbury, N.Y.: Feminist Press, 1982).

62. See Maureen Brady and Judith McDaniel, "Lesbians in the Mainstream: The Image of Lesbians in Recent Commercial Fiction," *Conditions* 6 (1979): 82–105.

hypocrisy, and hysteria in the heterosexual dialogue, for every heterosexual relationship is lived in the queasy strobe light of that lie. However we choose to identify ourselves, however we find ourselves labeled, it flickers across and distorts our lives.[63]

The lie keeps numberless women psychologically trapped, trying to fit mind, spirit, and sexuality into a prescribed script because they cannot look beyond the parameters of the acceptable. It pulls on the energy of such women even as it drains the energy of "closeted" lesbians—the energy exhausted in the double life. The lesbian trapped in the "closet," the woman imprisoned in prescriptive ideas of the "normal" share the pain of blocked options, broken connections, lost access to self-definition freely and powerfully assumed.

The lie is many-layered. In Western tradition, one layer—the romantic—asserts that women are inevitably, even if rashly and tragically, drawn to men; that even when that attraction is suicidal (e.g., *Tristan and Isolde,* Kate Chopin's *The Awakening*), it is still an organic imperative. In the tradition of the social sciences it asserts that primary love between the sexes is "normal"; that women *need* men as social and economic protectors, for adult sexuality, and for psychological completion; that the heterosexually constituted family is the basic social unit; that women who do not attach their primary intensity to men must be, in functional terms, condemned to an even more devastating outsiderhood than their outsiderhood as women. Small wonder that lesbians are reported to be a more hidden population than male homosexuals. The Black lesbian-feminist critic Lorraine Bethel, writing on Zora Neale Hurston, remarks that for a Black woman—already twice an outsider—to choose

63. See Russell and van de Ven, p. 40: "Few heterosexual women realize their lack of free choice about their sexuality, and few realize how and why compulsory heterosexuality is also a crime against them."

to assume still another "hated identity" is problematic indeed. Yet the lesbian continuum has been a life line for Black women both in Africa and the United States.

> Black women have a long tradition of bonding together . . . in a Black/women's community that has been a source of vital survival information, psychic and emotional support for us. We have a distinct Black woman-identified folk culture based on our experiences as Black women in this society; symbols, language and modes of expression that are specific to the realities of our lives. . . . Because Black women were rarely among those Blacks and females who gained access to literary and other acknowledged forms of artistic expression, this Black female bonding and Black woman-identification has often been hidden and unrecorded except in the individual lives of Black women through our own memories of our particular Black female tradition.[64]

Another layer of the lie is the frequently encountered implication that women turn to women out of hatred for men. Profound skepticism, caution, and righteous paranoia about men may indeed be part of any healthy woman's response to the misogyny of male-dominated culture, to the forms assumed by "normal" male sexuality, and to *the failure even of "sensitive" or "political" men to perceive or find these troubling.* Lesbian existence is also represented as mere refuge from male abuses, rather than as an electric and empowering charge between women. One of the most frequently quoted literary passages on lesbian relationship is that in which Colette's Renée, in *The Vagabond*, describes "the melancholy and touching image of two weak creatures who have perhaps found shelter in each other's arms, there to sleep and weep, safe from man who is often cruel, and there to taste *better than any pleasure, the bitter happiness of feeling themselves akin, frail*

64. Bethel, " 'This Infinity of Conscious Pain,' " *op. cit.*

and forgotten [emphasis added]."[65] Colette is often considered
a lesbian writer. Her popular reputation has, I think, much to
do with the fact that she writes about lesbian existence as if for
a male audience; her earliest "lesbian" novels, the Claudine
series, were written under compulsion for her husband and
published under both their names. At all events, except for her
writings on her mother, Colette is a less reliable source on the
lesbian continuum than, I would think, Charlotte Brontë, who
understood that while women may, indeed must, be one an-
other's allies, mentors, and comforters in the female struggle
for survival, there is quite extraneous delight in each other's
company and attraction to each others' minds and character,
which attend a recognition of each others' strengths.

By the same token, we can say that there is a *nascent* femi-
nist political content in the act of choosing a woman lover or
life partner in the face of institutionalized heterosexuality.[66]
But for lesbian existence to realize this political content in an
ultimately liberating form, the erotic choice must deepen and
expand into conscious woman identification—into lesbian fem-
inism.

The work that lies ahead, of unearthing and describing what
I call here "lesbian existence," is potentially liberating for all
women. It is work that must assuredly move beyond the limits
of white and middle-class Western Women's Studies to exam-
ine women's lives, work, and groupings within every racial,
ethnic, and political structure. There are differences, moreover,
between "lesbian existence" and the "lesbian continuum,"

65. Dinnerstein, the most recent writer to quote this passage, adds ominously: "But
what has to be added to her account is that these 'women enlaced' are sheltering each
other not just from what men want to do to them, but also from what they want to
do to each other" (Dinnerstein, p. 103). The fact is, however, that woman-to-woman
violence is a minute grain in the universe of male-against-female violence perpetuated
and rationalized in every social institution.
66. Conversation with Blanche W. Cook, New York City, March 1979.

differences we can discern even in the movement of our own lives. The lesbian continuum, I suggest, needs delineation in light of the "double life" of women, not only women self-described as heterosexual but also of self-described lesbians. We need a far more exhaustive account of the forms the double life has assumed. Historians need to ask at every point how heterosexuality as institution has been organized and maintained through the female wage scale, the enforcement of middle-class women's "leisure," the glamorization of so-called sexual liberation, the withholding of education from women, the imagery of "high art" and popular culture, the mystification of the "personal" sphere, and much else. We need an economics which comprehends the institution of heterosexuality, with its doubled workload for women and its sexual divisions of labor, as the most idealized of economic relations.

The question inevitably will arise: Are we then to condemn all heterosexual relationships, including those which are least oppressive? I believe this question, though often heartfelt, is the wrong question here. We have been stalled in a maze of false dichotomies which prevents our apprehending the institution as a whole: "good" versus "bad" marriages; "marriage for love" versus arranged marriage; "liberated" sex versus prostitution; heterosexual intercourse versus rape; *Liebeschmerz* versus humiliation and dependency. Within the institution exist, of course, qualitative differences of experience; but the absence of choice remains the great unacknowledged reality, and in the absence of choice, women will remain dependent upon the chance or luck of particular relationships and will have no collective power to determine the meaning and place of sexuality in their lives. As we address the institution itself, moreover, we begin to perceive a history of female resistance which has never fully understood itself because it has been so fragmented, miscalled, erased. It will require a courageous grasp of the politics and economics, as well as the cultural propaganda, of heterosexuality to carry us beyond individual cases or diversified group situations into the complex kind of overview needed to undo the power men everywhere wield over women, power which has become a model for every other form of exploitation and illegitimate control.

AFTERWORD

In 1980, Ann Snitow, Christine Stansell, and Sharon Thompson, three Marxist-feminist activists and scholars, sent out a call for papers for an anthology on the politics of sexuality. Having just finished writing "Compulsory Heterosexuality" for *Signs,* I sent them that manuscript and asked them to consider it. Their anthology, *Powers of Desire,* was published by the Monthly Review Press New Feminist Library in 1983 and included my paper. During the intervening period, the four of us were in correspondence, but I was able to take only limited advantage of this dialogue due to ill health and resulting surgery. With their permission, I reprint here excerpts from that correspondence as a way of indicating that my essay should be read as one contribution to a long exploration in progress, not as my own "last word" on sexual politics. I also refer interested readers to *Powers of Desire* itself.

Dear Adrienne,

. . . In one of our first letters, we told you that we were finding parameters of left-wing/feminist sexual discourse to be far broader than we imagined. Since then, we have perceived what we believe to be a crisis in the feminist movement about sex, an intensifying debate (although not always an explicit one), and a questioning of assumptions once taken for granted.

While we fear the link between sex and violence, as do Women Against Pornography, we wish we better understood its sources in ourselves as well as in men. In the Reagan era, we can hardly afford to romanticize any old norm of a virtuous and moral sexuality.

In your piece, you are asking the question, what would women choose in a world where patriarchy and capitalism did *not* rule? We agree with you that heterosexuality is an institution created between these grind stones, but we don't conclude, therefore, that it is entirely a male creation. You only allow for female historical agency insofar as women exist on the lesbian continuum while we would argue that women's history, like men's history, is created out of a dialectic of necessity and choice.

All three of us (hence one lesbian, two heterosexual women) had questions about your use of the term "false consciousness" for women's heterosexuality. In general, we think the false-consciousness model can blind us to the necessities and desires that comprise the lives of the oppressed. It can also lead to the too easy denial of others' experience when that experience is different from our own. We posit, rather, a complex social model in which all erotic life is a continuum, one which therefore includes relations with men.

Which brings us to this metaphor of the continuum. We know you are a poet, not an historian, and we look forward to reading your metaphors all our lives—and standing straighter as feminists, as women, for having read them. But the metaphor of the lesbian continuum is open to all kinds of misunderstandings, and these sometimes have odd political effects. For example, Sharon reports that at a recent meeting around the abortion-rights struggle, the notions of continuum arose in the discussion several times and underwent divisive transformation. Overall, the notion that two ways of being existed on the

same continuum was interpreted to mean that those two ways
were the *same*. The sense of range and gradation that your
description evokes disappeared. Lesbianism and female friend-
ship became exactly the same thing. Similarly, heterosexuality
and rape became the same. In one of several versions of the
continuum that evolved, a slope was added, like so:

Lesbianism
    ↘ Sex with men, no penetration
            ↘ Sex with men, penetration
                    ↘ Rape

This sloped continuum brought its proponents to the following
conclusion: An appropriate, workable abortion-rights strategy
is to inform all women that heterosexual penetration is rape,
whatever their subjective experience to the contrary. All
women will immediately recognize the truth of this and opt for
the alternative of nonpenetration. The abortion-rights struggle
will thus be simplified into a struggle against coercive sex and
its consequences (since no enlightened woman would voluntar-
ily undergo penetration unless her object was procreation—a
peculiarly Catholic-sounding view).

The proponents of this strategy were young women who
have worked hard in the abortion-rights movement for the past
two or more years. They are inexperienced but they are dedi-
cated. For this reason, we take their reading of your work
seriously. We don't think, however, that it comes solely, or
even at all, from the work itself. As likely a source is the
tendency to dichotomize that has plagued the women's move-
ment. The source of that tendency is harder to trace.

In that regard, the hints in "Compulsory" about the double
life of women intrigue us. You define the double life as "the
apparent acquiescence to an institution founded on male inter-

est and prerogative." But that definition doesn't really explain your other references—to, for instance, the "intense mixture" of love and anger in lesbian relationships and to the peril of romanticizing what it means "to love and act against the grain." We think these comments raise extremely important issues for feminists right now; the problem of division and anger among us needs airing and analysis. Is this, by any chance, the theme of a piece you have in the works?

. . . We would still love it if we could have a meeting with you in the next few months. Any chance? . . . Greetings and support from us—in all your undertakings.

We send love,
Sharon, Chris, and Ann

New York City
April 19, 1981

Dear Ann, Chris, and Sharon,

. . . It's good to be back in touch with you, you who have been so unfailingly patient, generous, and persistent. Above all, it's important to me that you know that ill health, not a withdrawal because of political differences, delayed my writing back to you. . . .

"False consciousness" can, I agree, be used as a term of dismissal for any thinking we don't like or adhere to. But, as I tried to illustrate in some detail, there is a real, identifiable system of heterosexual propaganda, of defining women as existing for the sexual use of men, which goes beyond "sex role" or "gender" stereotyping or "sexist imagery" to include a vast number of verbal and nonverbal messages. And this I call "control of consciousness." The possibility of a woman who does not exist sexually for men—the lesbian possibility—is buried, erased, occluded, distorted, misnamed, and driven un-

derground. The feminist books—Chodorow, Dinnerstein, Eh-
renreich and English, and others—which I discuss at the begin-
ning of my essay contribute to this invalidation and erasure,
and as such are part of the problem.

My essay is founded on the belief that we all think from
within the limits of certain solipsisms—usually linked with
privilege, racial, cultural, and economic as well as sexual—
which present themselves as "the universal," "the way things
are," "all women," etc., etc. I wrote it equally out of the belief
that in becoming conscious of our solipsisms we have certain
kinds of choices, that we can and must re-educate ourselves. I
never have maintained that heterosexual feminists are walking
about in a state of "brainwashed" false consciousness. Nor have
such phrases as "sleeping with the enemy" seemed to me either
profound or useful. *Homophobia* is too diffuse a term and does
not go very far in helping us identify and talk about the sexual
solipsism of heterosexual feminism. In this paper I was trying
to ask heterosexual feminists to examine their experience of
heterosexuality critically and antagonistically, to critique the
institution of which they are a part, to struggle with the norm
and its implications for women's freedom, to become more
open to the considerable resources offered by the lesbian-femi-
nist perspective, to refuse to settle for the personal privilege
and solution of the individual "good relationship" within the
institution of heterosexuality.

As regards "female historical agency," I wanted, precisely,
to suggest that the victim model is insufficient; that there *is* a
history of female agency and choice which has actually chal-
lenged aspects of male supremacy; that, like male supremacy,
these can be found in many different cultures. . . . It's not that
I think all female agency has been solely and avowedly lesbian.
But by erasing lesbian existence from female history, from
theory, from literary criticism . . . from feminist approaches to

economic structure, ideas about "the family," etc., an enormous amount of female agency is kept unavailable, hence unusable. I wanted to demonstrate that that kind of obliteration continues to be acceptable in seriously regarded feminist texts. What surprised me in the responses to my essay, including your notes, is how almost every aspect of it has been considered, except this—to me—central one. I was taking a position which was neither lesbian/separatist in the sense of dismissing heterosexual women nor a "gay civil rights" plea for . . . openness to lesbianism as an "option" or an "alternate life style." I was urging that lesbian *existence* has been an unrecognized and unaffirmed claiming by women of their sexuality, thus a pattern of resistance, thus also a kind of borderline position from which to analyze and challenge the relationship of heterosexuality to male supremacy. And that lesbian existence, when recognized, demands a conscious restructuring of feminist analysis and criticism, not just a token reference or two.

I certainly agree with you that the term *lesbian continuum* can be misused. It was, in the example you report of the abortion-rights meeting, though I would think anyone who had read my work from *Of Woman Born* onward would know that my position on abortion and sterilization abuse is more complicated than that. My own problem with the phrase is that it can be, is, used by women who have not yet begun to examine the privileges and solipsisms of heterosexuality, as a safe way to describe their felt connections with women, without having to share in the risks and threats of lesbian existence. What I had thought to delineate rather complexly as a continuum has begun to sound more like "life-style shopping." *Lesbian continuum* —the phrase—came from a desire to allow for the greatest possible variation of female-identified experience, while paying a different kind of respect to *lesbian existence*— the traces and knowledge of women who have made their primary erotic and emotional choices for women. If I were writing the paper today, I would still want to make this distinction, but would put more caveats around *lesbian continuum*. I fully agree with you that Smith-Rosenberg's "female world" is not a social ideal, enclosed as it is within prescriptive middle-class heterosexuality and marriage.

My own essay could have been stronger had it drawn on more of the literature by Black women toward which Toni Morrison's *Sula* inevitably pointed me. In reading a great deal more of Black women's fiction I began to perceive a different set of valences from those found in white women's fiction for the most part: a different quest for the woman hero, a different relationship both to sexuality with men and to female loyalty and bonding. . . .

You comment briefly on your reactions to some of the radical-feminist works I cited in my first footnote.[67] I am myself critical of some of them even as I found them vitally useful. What most of them share is a taking seriously of misogyny—of organized, institutionalized, normalized hostility and violence against women. I feel no "hierarchy of oppressions" is needed in order for us to take misogyny as seriously as we take racism, anti-Semitism, imperialism. To take misogyny seriously needn't mean that we perceive women merely as victims, without responsibilities or choices; it does mean recognizing the "necessity" in that "dialectic of necessity and choice"—identifying, describing, refusing to turn aside our eyes. I think that some of the apparent reductiveness, or even obsessiveness, of some white radical-feminist theory derives from racial and/or class solipsism, but also from the immense effort of trying to render woman hating visible amid so much denial. . . .

Finally, as to poetry and history: I want both in my life; I

67. See note 9, above, pp. 30–31.

need to see through both. If metaphor can be misconstrued, history can also lead to misconstrual when it obliterates acts of resistance or rebellion, wipes out transformational models, or sentimentalizes power relationships. I know you know this. I believe we are all trying to think and write out of our best consciences, our most open consciousness. I expect that quality in this book which you are editing, and look forward with anticipation to the thinking—and the actions—toward which it may take us.

> In sisterhood,
> Adrienne

Montague, Massachusetts
November 1981

Disobedience and Women's Studies (1981)

For those of you who are unaware of it, I want to start with the fact that the advance coverage of this convention by the *Hartford Courant* on May 19, 1981, was headlined "Lesbian Housing Available for Women's Conference at UConn" and focused entirely on the arrangements for a "lesbian section" of the dormitory, where "between 60 and 75 women" would by request be lodged. Heavy emphasis was laid on alleged difficulties between lesbians and heterosexual women last year in Bloomington and on the issue of "segregated" housing. There was no mention whatsoever of racism as the theme of the convention.

I feel it is important to start by analyzing this. It is, first of all, a deliberate erasure of our declared purpose here. The National Women's Studies Association chose, as a part of the feminist movement rather than as a dutiful daughter of academia, to address the estrangement, ignorance, fear, anger, and

Keynote address for the National Women's Studies Association Convention, Storrs, Connecticut, 1981. The theme of the convention was "Women Respond to Racism." See also Audre Lorde, "The Uses of Anger," in Sister Outsider *(Trumansburg, N.Y.: Crossing Press, 1984). Both keynote addresses were first published in* Women's Studies Quarterly 9, no. 3 *(Fall 1981).*

disempowerment created by the institutional racism which saturates all our lives. Many of us have come here in a mixture of hope and fear, hope and anger, hope and determination. Many, it may be assumed, have stayed away: some for lack of money, some for lack of hope, some for lack of determination, some for lack of caring. But these meetings have a purpose, and this purpose, visibly stated in NWSA's literature, has been wiped out by the local press.

It should be obvious to us by now that this kind of erasure serves and supports the racism of the larger society. Over and over in the past, women have met or tried to meet across barriers of color and lines of privilege, only to have those efforts erased in the historical record and the academic curriculum. We thus lack transformational models and the evidence that what we are trying to do has a history with its own mistakes and advances from which we could learn. Even more, the woman of color herself has been obliterated from the record. To quote from the title of a forthcoming collection edited by Patricia Bell Scott, Barbara Smith, and Gloria Hull: *All the Women Are White, All the Blacks Are Men, but Some of Us Are Brave.* [1] How simple, then, for the *Hartford Courant* to erase the issue of racism, in a state where the Ku Klux Klan openly marches, by playing on a different string of bigotry and fear—the New Right's vocal anti-feminism and homophobia. How easy, as well, for these tactics to touch the strings both of homophobia and of racism in the enclave of Women's Studies itself, where lesbians are still feared and women of color are still ignored.

It would be very easy—given the demands of the task NWSA has set itself here—for us to lose our hard-won threads

1. Gloria T. Hull, Patricia Bell Scott, and Barbara Smith, eds., *All the Women Are White, All the Blacks Are Men, but Some of Us Are Brave: Black Women's Studies* (Old Westbury, N.Y.: Feminist Press, 1982).

of connectedness and purpose, to focus, as the media intend us to do, on *their* choice of agenda for us. But we don't have to do this. We can choose to see the connections between what is being floodlighted, targeted, on the one hand, and what is being rendered invisible, on the other. White feminists and lesbians are not, on the whole, immediately identifiable: they have to be pointed out. Women of color are, on the whole, identifiable; but they aren't supposed to be here anyway, so their presence, and whatever we have in common as women, must be erased from the record. White women who seem to be crossing the lines drawn for them by the white fathers must be targeted so they can be ordered back behind those lines; the white community must understand that these women are not acting like their fathers' daughters. Women of color who are found in the wrong place as defined at any given time by the white fathers will receive their retribution unseen: if they are beaten, raped, insulted, harassed, mutilated, murdered, these events will go unreported, unpunished, unconnected; and white women are not even supposed to know they occur, let alone identify with the sufferings endured.

There is a word which has been resounding in my head for several months, since I first read it on the cover of the southern lesbian-feminist journal *Feminary:* that word is *disobedience.* (The latest issue of *Feminary* is devoted to that theme.)[2] And in thinking about this week of meetings of NWSA, it has seemed to me that disobedience is what NWSA is potentially about, in choosing to build a conference around women's response to racism. The question now facing Women's Studies, it seems to me, is the extent to which she has, in the past decade, matured into the dutiful daughter of the white, patriar-

2. *Feminary: A Lesbian Journal for the South* 2, nos. 1 and 2 (1981).

chal university—a daughter who threw tantrums and played the tomboy when she was younger but who has now learned to wear a dress and speak and act almost as nicely as Daddy wants her to; the extent to which Women's Studies will remember that her mother was not Athena, but the Women's Liberation movement of the 1960s, a movement blazing with lesbian energy, whose earliest journals had names like *It Ain't Me, Babe, No More Fun and Games, off our backs, Up from Under,* and *The Furies.* In other words, how disobedient will Women's Studies be in the 1980s: how will this Association address the racism, misogyny, homophobia of the university and of the corporate and militarist society in which it is embedded; how will white feminist scholars and teachers and students practice disobedience to patriarchy?

In that same issue of *Feminary* in an essay on "Rebellion," Minnie Bruce Pratt writes the following:

> I had fantasized about the Great Rebellion [the southern term for the Civil War] because I wanted some vicarious motion, change, control of my life, but this was a delusive daydream, one that white people of the old Confederacy have been caught in since before the War, the daydream, the romance of rebellion, the breaking out of the nightmare of slavery, race hatred, economic differences, sex differences; . . . this was a romance because the act of rebellion satisfied the need for change while the values which were defended, those of white male supremacy, remained the same. . . . I understood years later that my mother and grandmothers and great-grandmothers had been heroines, in one way, and had used their will to grit their teeth and endure, to walk through the ruins, blood, and mess left by men. I understood finally that this heroic will to endure is still not the same as the will to change, the true rebellion.[3]

3. Minnie Bruce Pratt, "Rebellion," *Feminary* 3, nos. 1 and 2 (1981): 6–20.

To understand where as white women we have been situated in the overall system of oppression which also oppresses us is crucial knowledge if we are serious about our lives. Pratt's essay is really about the difference between true and false rebellion. False rebellion is to varying degrees in varying places acceptable to the white fathers. True rebellion is something that, with each step we take, cuts us further off from identification with racist patriarchy, which has rewarded us for our loyalty and which will punish us for becoming disloyal. It does not matter how we change our names or what music we listen to, or whether we celebrate Christmas or Hanukkah or the solstice, or how many books by women we teach. So long as we can identify only with white women, we are still connected to that system of objectification and callousness and cruelty called racism. And that system is not simply a "patriarchal mind-fuck," an idea, which the feminist can assume she has tossed out along with "mankind" and God the Father. It is a material reality of the flesh and nerves, and our relation to it as white feminists is a complex function. As the Black writer/activist Michele Russell writes in her "Open Letter to the Academy," addressing white women in the university:

> Your oppression and exploitation have been more cleverly masked than ours, more delicately elaborated. The techniques, refined. You were rewarded in minor ways for docile and active complicity in our dehumanization. At base, the risk of your complete alienation from the system of white male rule that also exploited you was too great to run. The perpetuation of the race depended upon your reproductive capacity: your willingness to bear and rear succeeding generations of oppressors. While your reproductive function has been the only reason for your relative protection in the colonizing process, ours, on the contrary, has sharpened the knife colonialism applies to our throats and wombs. Witness government-sanctioned mass sterilization in Puerto Rico, New York, and Brazil.

And in thinking of the issue of enforced sterilization, we must also inevitably think of the issue of NWSA's position on the presence of, and funding by, agencies such as AID (Agency for International Development). Russell continues, still addressing white women scholars:

> I draw on these discrepancies in our condition not to assign blame or to suggest that you are blind to the implications of this process. We also know that history is full of examples of white women rejecting the cultural and economic blackmail that kept you in service. You walked out on your jobs: in the home, in mills and mines, in heavy manufacturing, in bureaucracies. Occasionally, small minorities succeeded in creating artistic and intellectual communities that sustained elements of a culture independent of the dominant commodity relations of bourgeois society. But on balance, that history—the one of your resistance—is still to be discovered and amplified by this generation. All of you. That is why you are important.
>
> The central question, of course, is "What version of civilization will you construct?" What stories will you tell each other and leave for future generations? What truths will consistently inform your plot? How will you define yourselves in relation to the central patterns of domination in the world, and how will you align on the side of freedom? How rigorously will you face your own past with all its warts?[4]

Only as white women begin to understand both our obedience and complicity, *and* our rebellions, do we begin to have

4. Michele Russell, "An Open Letter to the Academy," in Bunch *et al.*, eds., *Building Feminist Theory: Essays from "Quest, A Feminist Quarterly"* (New York and London: Longman, 1981), pp. 101–110.

[A.R., 1986: For references on government-sanctioned sterilization abuse, see Adrienne Rich, *On Lies, Secrets, and Silence: Selected Prose, 1966–1978* (New York: W. W. Norton, 1979), p. 266; Committee for Abortion Rights and against Sterilization Abuse, "Women under Attack: Abortion, Sterilization Abuse, and Reproductive Freedom" (1979); Thomas M. Shapiro, *Population Control Politics: Women, Sterilization and Reproductive Choice* (Philadelphia: Temple University Press, 1985).]

the tools for an ongoing response to racism which is neither circular, rhetorical, nor resentful. White women's anti-racism and lesbianism have both been profound refusals to obey.

It seems to me that the word *guilt* has arisen too often in discussions such as these. Women of color in their anger are charged with provoking guilt in white women; white women accuse each other of provoking guilt; it is guilt, endlessly, that is supposed to stand between white women and disobedience, white women and true rebellion. I have come to wonder if guilt, with its connotations of being emotionally overwhelmed and bullied, or paralyzed, is not more a form of defensive resentment or self-protection than an authentic response to the past and its warts. Guilt does not move, guilt does not look you in the eye, guilt does not speak a personal language. I would like to ask every white woman who feels that her guilt is being provoked in discussions of racism to consider what uses she has for this guilt and how it uses her, and to decide for herself if a guilt-ridden feminism, a guilt-ridden rebellion, sounds like a viable way of life.

Each of us surely needs to know that no other white woman has any competitive monopoly on understanding racism. Each of us needs other white women as allies in meeting the immense rush of forces which are stirred up at the mention of something we are not supposed even to think about: how we as victims of objectification have objectified other women, what rewards we have reaped from our obedience, and what our present and future responsibility must be.

Finally, I want to say something about my personal understanding of racism. For a long time, particularly in the 1960s, I needed to believe that, though white, I was not a carrier of racism. If, as a political choice, I was engaged in teaching Asian and Black and Puerto Rican freshmen instead of white graduate-school poets; if I joined in the fight for open admissions at the City University; if a kind of nobility and heroism my spirit craved had become opened to me through King's "Letter from Birmingham Jail," Baldwin's essays, the letters of George Jackson; if the words of Frantz Fanon and Malcolm X felt cathartic and cleansing to me, why did those words also feel accusing and menacing? What in me felt accused or threatened, even while something else in me felt those words as a life line of sanity?

The white male Left offered no answers. The racists were all "out there": the pigs, the rednecks, the reactionary bourgeois professors, Nelson Rockefeller, the generically "Jewish" landlords. The racists were my parents, my southern family, not those whites who marched singing "We Shall Overcome," and certainly not anyone white who had worked in the early days with SNCC or traveled to Mississippi. Credentials were important—particularly a Black lover, a Black child—as if they could solve, once and for all, the problem of how and when, if ever, the white person stopped thinking racist thoughts or seeing in racist patterns; became washed clean, as it were; became "part of the solution instead of the problem." There was a very "born again" spirit among white anti-racist activists in the 1960s—as if they could discard their pasts, as if they must, having once seen the political light, have no fear or hatred of darkness anywhere in their souls.

I speak of that period because it has been part of the history I have needed to face rigorously, in particular as a feminist committed to the struggle of all women for liberation. I think we need to get rid of the useless baggage that says that by opposing racist violence, by doing anti-racist work, or by becoming feminists white women somehow cease to carry racism within them.

The southern white lesbian novelist Cris South writes, "The roots may be in the patriarchy but they've grown into us." What *was* true for me was that in growing into feminism and coming out as a lesbian I found a sense of personal and collective history and identity, affirmed by the words of white women who had struggled in the past for justice and freedom *as women:* the Grimké sisters, Susan B. Anthony, Olive Schreiner, Emma Goldman, Virginia Woolf, to name a few. Feminism became a political and spiritual base from which I could move to examine rather than try to hide my own racism, recognize that I have anti-racist work to do continuously within myself. Increasingly, the writings of contemporary lesbian and feminist women of color have moved and challenged me to push my horizons further, examine with fresh eyes the world I thought I knew and took for granted. There is an inner tension and dynamic I need to acknowledge between my beliefs and standards for myself, and how I still think and act as a daughter of white patriarchy. If I say that I am trying to recognize and change in myself certain failures to see or hear, certain kinds of arrogance, ignorance, passivity, which have to do with living in a white skin—that is, which have to do with racism—I can say this as a woman committed to the love of women, including love for myself.

Toward a More Feminist Criticism (1981)

I come to this task as a writer in need of criticism, as a student
of literature who also sometimes writes criticism, as co-editor
of a small lesbian-feminist journal, *Sinister Wisdom,* and as a
member of the community of feminist and/or lesbian editors,
printers, booksellers, publishers, archivists, and reviewers who
met in Washington, D.C., several weekends ago, defining our-
selves as "Women in Print." It is especially out of that commu-
nity that I wish to speak, and much of what I shall bring
together here I have absorbed from and with other lesbian and
feminist members of that community in the process of trying
to address issues of survival. As the first call for that conference
stated: *The survival of the women's movement, as of any revolu-
tionary movement, depends directly on that of our communica-
tions network.* The need for more and better criticism as a part
of that network was one theme in our discussions.

It strikes me that at present there are really two kinds of
self-defined feminist criticism being done. One originates in
the universities, usually in Women's Studies, and addresses

*Opening address, Feminist Studies in Literature Symposium, University of
Minnesota, Minneapolis, 1981.*

that community primarily; it concentrates on works of the past which can most readily be included within an already existing canon or on contemporary works which are published by commercial presses. The other, though sometimes written by women with university degrees, is grounded in the larger feminist community with its increasing consciousness of diversity and the ensuing differences of tone, language, style. The first kind of criticism tends to be published in journals like *Signs, Women's Studies, Feminist Studies* as well as now and then in nonfeminist literary and critical journals like *College English, Parnassus,* and professional quarterlies. The second tends to appear in magazines like *Conditions, Feminary, The Feminist Review, off our backs, Sinister Wisdom,* as well as in such journals as *First World, Radical Teacher, Freedomways, Southern Exposure,* etc. The trouble is that the first kind of criticism is not listening to the second—is in fact drawing back from the second. It is this schism that I want to examine here.

I'd like to begin by noting that there is a well-known split in Western literary culture between a literary "establishment" which represents middle-class and traditional values, and an "avant-garde" which has seen itself variously as challenging entrenched ideas and forms, flouting the rules, "smashing the iamb," publishing "little" magazines in opposition to the current establishment mode. Sometimes, but not always, the literary "avant-garde" has been politically radical as well; sometimes (as with the Fugitive movement in the South, which rapidly became an establishment) it has reflected conservative to fascistic political attitudes within a "modernist" or formally rebellious aesthetic. Feminist criticism began not as a school of literary criticism but as a politically motivated act of looking at literature, both by men and by women, in terms of *sexual politics,* as Kate Millett named her landmark book in 1970. In her preface Millett wrote:

This essay, composed of equal parts of literary and cultural criticism, is something of an anomaly, a hybrid, possibly a new mutation altogether. I have operated on the premise that there is room for a criticism which takes into account the larger cultural context in which literature is conceived and produced. Criticism which originates from literary history is too limited in scope to do this; criticism which originates in aesthetic considerations, "New Criticism," never wished to do so.[1]

Feminist criticism grew out of a Women's Liberation movement which took seriously the work of critiquing *all* of culture, from beauty pageants to university texts, in terms of its reflection of, and impact on, women's lives. In her 1977 essay "Toward a Black Feminist Criticism," Barbara Smith reminds us all that

for books to be real and remembered they have to be talked about. For books to be understood they must be examined in such a way that the basic intentions of the writers are at least considered. . . . Before the advent of specifically feminist criticism in this decade, books by white women. . . . were not clearly perceived as the cultural manifestation of an oppressed people. It took the surfacing of the second wave of the North American feminist movement to expose the fact that these works contain a stunningly accurate record of the impact of patriarchal values and practice upon the lives of women and more significantly that literature by white women provides essential insights into female experience.[2]

With this statement in mind, I would define a feminist literary criticism as a criticism which is consciously involved in a movement for women's liberation—indeed, a revolutionary

1. Kate Millett, *Sexual Politics* (Garden City, N.Y.: Doubleday, 1970), p. xii.
2. Barbara Smith, "Toward a Black Feminist Criticism," in *All the Women Are White, All the Blacks Are Men, but Some of Us Are Brave: Black Women's Studies*, ed. Gloria T. Hull, Patricia Bell Scott, and Barbara Smith (Old Westbury, N.Y.: Feminist Press, 1982), p. 154.

movement. I would not define as feminist literary criticism simply the writing by a woman about other women's books without consciousness of the political context of women's writing; or by an author who perceives herself as merely participating in some female "alternative reading" in a liberal supermarket of the intellect; or by one who accepts the parameters of whiteness, heterosexuality, and academic scholarship as furnishing an essentially complete view of things. I would like to invoke a definition of feminist criticism which implies continuous and conscious accountability to the lives of women—not only those women who read and write books or are working, however tenuously, in academic settings. For white feminists, who make up by far the largest group of academic feminists, this involves deliberately trying to unlearn the norm of universal whiteness, which is the norm of the culture of academia and of the dominant culture beyond; it also and equally means trying to unlearn the norm of universal heterosexuality. It means that we do not attribute to our work an inclusiveness it does not possess, that we don't rest satisfied with ritualistically tacking on a chapter or a paragraph or a footnote alluding to women of color and/or lesbians. To challenge the universality of whiteness and heterosexuality implies as radical and astonishing a process as many of us went through over a decade ago in challenging patriarchal values and practice. It is, I believe, the next unavoidable step that feminist criticism must make— and it is already beginning.

In looking at literary criticism by white academic feminists, I am often surprised at the wealth of reading cited from the works of white male critics and at how often there goes along with this a tone of defensiveness, of needing to argue with these gentlemen, of being still somewhat enmeshed in dialogues which serve to isolate the feminist as a woman rather than connect her with a larger community of women. I can feel a kind of underlying strain, too, the strain of trying to explain oneself yet again when one needs to be moving on—the strain of trying bravely to carry the banner of feminism high in a hostile setting, trying to exchange collegial banter without perceptible "bitterness," bringing into play a panoply of terms and methods learned in the classrooms of lit. crit., all the time using women writers—mostly white—as the "texts" to be treated. I know this strain very well in myself, as a white and middle-class woman who lived for years as a heterosexual in academia. It is the strain of trying to have it both ways, be both pleasing and bold, the token straining not to act like a token. (I cannot help but recognize how much of this I've done myself or am still capable of doing.)

I want to ask the feminist critic of literature to inform herself not just with training in literary exegesis but in a concrete and grounded knowledge of the feminist movement— which means reading not only books by women, but feminist newspapers, periodicals, pamphlets, articles; studies on woman battering, welfare mothers, sexual and economic struggles in the workplace, compulsory sterilization, incest, women in prison; resources from the feminist presses like the *Fight Back!* anthology on feminist resistance to male violence, published here in Minneapolis by Cleis Press; or *This Bridge Called My Back: Writings by Radical Women of Color,* edited by Cherríe Moraga and Gloria Anzaldúa and published by Persephone Press; or *Top Ranking: Racism and Classism in the Lesbian Community,* published by February 3 Press; or J. R. Roberts's *Black Lesbians: An Annotated Bibliography,* published by Naiad Press. I want to ask her to consider her work a potential resource also, a resource *for us,* for our movement; to see herself not as writing just for other critics and scholars, but to help make books both "real and remembered," to stir ordinary women to read what they might otherwise miss or avoid, to help us all sort through which words, in Lillian Smith's phrase, chain us and which can set us free. In a provocative recent piece of feminist criticism, which is grounded in this way, Jan Clausen suggests that the striking role of poetry and poets in the movement has led some women to attribute too much power to words and language, to elevate the poet rather than the organizer or practical strategist to the role of spokeswoman. "Feminism desperately needs actions as well as words," she says.[3] I share Clausen's uneasiness about a movement infatuated with language to the neglect of action. I share it particularly because I am a poet who often finds herself assigned the role of spokeswoman. Some of us are increasingly concerned about the level of ritual assent accorded to our poetic language—"assent without credence," as a friend once defined it, to my own relief; about the frustration of being listened to, written about, objectified, perhaps, but not heard —at least in any sense of hearing which might bear on action. Even to be able to express this in public is a measure of how harshly I have felt the experience of applause and accolade without discrimination or true on-going critical response. It's not that I believe in a direct line of response, from a poem to an action: I'm not convinced that such a connection would be desirable or that the poet necessarily knows what action is needed. In fact, it may be action that leads to poetry, the deed to the word, when the poet identifies with others like and unlike herself who are trying to transform an oppressive order. But I do believe that words *can* help us move or keep us paralyzed, and that our choices of language and verbal tone have something—a great deal—to do with how we live our lives and whom we end up speaking with and hearing; and that we can deflect words, by trivialization, of course, but also by ritual-

3. Jan Clausen, *A Movement of Poets,* pamphlet (Brooklyn, N.Y.: Long Haul, 1981).

ized respect, or we can let them enter our souls and mix with the juices of our minds.

And the critique of language needs to come not just from women who define themselves as writers but from women who will test the work against their experience—who, like Woolf's "common reader," are interested in literature as a key to life, not an escape from it. I think that every feminist poet must long—I do—for real criticism of her work—not just descriptive, but analytical criticism which takes her language and images seriously enough to question them, as Susan Wood-Thompson questioned my use of images of blindness in a review in the southern lesbian-feminist journal *Feminary*. I also need to know when in my work I am merely doing well what I know well how to do and when I am avoiding certain expressive risks. And while I can count on friends for some of this, it would be better for all feminist writers if such principled criticism were to come also from strangers—it would broaden the field in which we are working.

But this kind of criticism implies a commitment not just to literature but to readers, and not just to women who are readers here and now but to widening the possibility of reading and writing for women to whom books have been closed. In her beautiful and thought-provoking essay "Researching Alice Dunbar-Nelson," the Black critic Gloria T. Hull describes her search for a new way of writing as a feminist scholar, visualizing the diverse kinds of readers she wants to address, from parents, brothers, lovers, to academic colleagues to other Black feminists, trying to create "organic" articles "rather than write sneaky, schizophrenic essays from under two or three different hats."[4] In this particular essay, Hull describes her work with

4. Gloria T. Hull, "Researching Alice Dunbar-Nelson," in *All the Women Are White*, pp. 193–194.

the manuscript collection preserved by Dunbar-Nelson's surviving niece, the dynamics of her relationship with the niece herself, and the meaning of this work and its discoveries for Hull personally and for the study of Black women writers in general. Toward the end of the essay she formulates some principles for a Black feminist critical methodology. I want to cite them here:

(1) everything about the subject is important for a total understanding and analysis of her life and work; (2) the proper scholarly stance is engaged rather than "objective"; (3) the personal (both the subject's and the critic's) *is* political; (4) description must be accompanied by analysis; (5) consciously maintaining the angle of vision of a person who is both Black and female is imperative; as is the necessity for a class-conscious, anti-capitalist perspective; (6) being principled requires rigorous truthfulness and "telling it all" [here Hull is alluding, among other things, to her discovery, in editing Dunbar-Nelson's diary, of her lesbian relationships]; (7) research/criticism is not an academic/intellectual game, but a pursuit with social meanings rooted in the "real world." I had always proceeded from the assumption that Dunbar-Nelson had much to say to us and, even more importantly, that dealing honestly with her could, in a more-than-metaphoric sense, "save" some Black woman's life—as being able to write in this manner about her had, in a very concrete way, "saved" my own.[5]

And so the question hangs before us: Can a truly feminist criticism be carried on within the university or for academic publications, and if so, how? What does it mean, for example, that my own work can be respectfully quoted and discussed in academic classrooms and in articles without acknowledging that it is the work of a lesbian, where lesbians are never men-

5. *Ibid.*, p. 193.

tioned? And what does it mean that, several years after Barbara Smith's "Toward a Black Feminist Criticism" and Alice Walker's essay/meditation "One Child of One's Own," and over a year after *Signs* published my essay "Compulsory Heterosexuality and Lesbian Existence," the current issue of *Signs* can open with a lengthy article which makes strong claims for feminist thought as "rethinking thinking itself" and discusses a number of recent books of academic feminist criticism, all white-centered and heterosexist, without the slightest comment on that fact?[6] How is it possible that a similarly ambitious article, published in *Feminist Studies*, can "discuss a 'feminist literary criticism' without reference to the work of women of color and/or identifiable lesbians"?[7] What does it mean about the very terms, the structures with which the critic tries to conceptualize her ideas, when she tries to build an exhaustive theory merely on one limited, white, heterosexual slice of experience and reading? What does it mean about how seriously the white academic feminist critic reads the work of an Alice Walker, a Barbara Smith, an Elly Bulkin, a Michele Russell, a Toni Cade Bambara? Does she read the journals in which she might find their criticism—such as *Conditions, First World, Freedomways, Radical Teacher, Sinister Wisdom;* or does she, as a literary critic, feel it more important to keep up with *Partisan Review, Critical Inquiry, Semiotics,* and the journals emanating from half a dozen English departments, thus imbibing not only their measure of what counts but their language? Why *is* the language of much academic feminist criticism so ultra-cool, so bright, so spruce and polished? Gloria T. Hull

6. Myra Jehlen, "Archimedes and the Paradox of Feminist Criticism," *Signs: Journal of Women in Culture and Society* 6, no. 4 (Summer 1981): 571–600.

7. Judith Gardiner, Elly Bulkin, Rena Grasso Patterson, and Annette Kolodny, "An Interchange on Feminist Criticism: On 'Dancing through the Minefield,'" *Feminist Studies* 8, no. 3 (Fall 1982): 636.

speaks of the kind of style she has consciously rejected as a
Black feminist critic:

> Probably as an (over?) reaction to the condescending, witty but
> empty, British urbanity of tone which is the hallmark of traditional
> white male literary scholarship (and which I dislike intensely) I
> usually discuss Dunbar-Nelson with level high seriousness—and
> always with caring.[8]

Essential for the feminist critic who believes that her work
is "a pursuit with social meanings rooted in the 'real world' "
is a clear understanding of power: of how culture, as meted out
in the university, works to empower some and disempower
others; of how she herself may be writing out of a situation of
unexamined privilege, whether of skin color, heterosexuality,
economic and educational background, or other. For example,
if I write (as I have done) on fiction by Black women, it must
be clear to me that my interpretation of that fiction is that of
a white, middle-class, Jewish lesbian feminist—a complex view
but not an authoritative one; that I have, being white, no
special overview which allows me to speak with any authority
beyond trying to describe what the effect and impression of
this literature has been on me, and why I think it valuable for
other white women. Even so, I am probably going to be taken
more seriously in some quarters than the Black woman scholar
whose combined experience and research give her far more
penetrating knowledge and awareness than mine. I will be
taken more seriously because I am white, because though a
lesbian I am often willfully not perceived as such, and because
the invisibility of the woman of color who is the scholar/critic
or the poet *or* the novelist is part of the structure of *my*
privilege, even my credibility.

8. Hull, pp. 193–194.

No one is suggesting that the woman with all or many of the privileges of white skin, heterosexuality, class background is thereby disqualified from writing and criticizing. However, I believe she has a responsibility not to read, think, write, and act as if all women had the same privileges, or to assume that privilege confers some kind of special vision. She has a responsibility to be as clear as possible about the compromises she makes, about her own fear and trembling as she sits down to write; to admit her limitations when she picks up work by women who write from a very different culture and sourcement, to admit to feelings of confusion and being out of her depth. We need to support each other in rejecting the limitations of a tradition—a manner of reading, of speaking, of writing, of criticizing—which was never really designed to include us at all.

From the perspective of that tradition, of the academy, of course, other questions can be and are daily raised. *Aren't you trying to make literature accountable to the winds of political change? Aren't politics and art always disastrous bedfellows? Are feminist critics supposed to judge works by some party line of political correctness, whatever the writer's personal intentions?* But these questions are not as pure, as politically neutral, as they seem to be: they spring from the dominant white male culture, a culture profoundly hostile to the self-definition and self-love of people of color, and/or poor people, and/or white women, and/or lesbians and gay men. *Can art be political and still be timeless? All* art is political in terms of who was allowed to make it, what brought it into being, why and how it entered the canon, and why we are still discussing it.

I believe that when we posit a movement of women, a movement both conscious of our oppression as women and profoundly aware of differences among us, a true Women's Liberation movement, we enter a realm more complex than we have moved in before, so that the very questions about literature become new questions. When the Black feminist critic Mary Helen Washington, in her anthology of fiction by and about Black women, *Midnight Birds,* includes a single story by a Black lesbian (never identified as such) and makes no reference to the existence of Black lesbians in her foreword, she is limiting the questions she as critic can ask. When a white feminist critic merely tacks on women of color to her analysis as a separate chapter or footnote, or erases their existence altogether, she is not simply omitting but distorting, and the organic fabric of her criticism is weakened by these distortions. When she deliberately tries to work from a point of view that is *not* white solipsist, she will feel her analysis changing; she is going to see differently and further, not just about the writings of women of color but also about the writings of white women. The consciousness of racism and homophobia does not mean simply trying to excise racist language or homophobic stereotypes (though that is a necessary beginning); it does mean working to see the field with a fresh vision, to experience whiteness or heterosexuality as relative states and not as authoritative positions. But this can be upsetting: it makes us hear things we didn't use to hear, feel split between familiar and emergent parts of ourselves; it makes us question unexamined loyalties; it is not conducive to pleasant collegiality and banter; it makes us reread our own past writings with impatience; it changes the list of issues we thought it important to explore; and it has everything to do with what we find in literature.

During a couple of workshops at the Women in Print conference I felt that I was hearing a new kind of literature described, a literature desired and needed, yet still uncreated. Women of color and white women talked of the possibility of learning, whether as authors of fiction or as reviewers, to look from the angle of women unlike ourselves. How much do our differences mitigate what we hold in common as women? We talked of how the critic or reviewer needs to develop a clear sense of her own political and cultural identity, and locate herself honestly in relation to the work she attempts to criticize. How the imaginative writer could learn to write with accountability of women who are not simply of her own caste or class or background, resisting stereotypes, trying to create whole persons—and how this may mean changing her life, not just her writing. We talked of the urge to create literary superwomen, whether dark-skinned or lesbian or both, to make up for years of invisibility or degrading portrayals in literature, and the need to reject feminist versions of "socialist realism." In one workshop, two blind white lesbians, one Puerto Rican lesbian, one Black lesbian, and one white working-class lesbian spoke of wanting to find themselves and women like them in literature—"not always in the foreground either, but in the background too, as just part of the scene, if we can be treated seriously there," as one woman put it. We began to imagine a poetic language, a prose language, which was free of stereotypes—whether of dark or light, or of disability or age, or body image—which was beyond frozen, reductive, repetitive image making. We began to talk as if one task of the critic might be to keep such possibilities before us, both as readers and as writers.

When I was an undergraduate English major, there were a number of "major critical texts" in the English language, written by English men and considered indispensable: Sidney's "A Defense of Poetry"; Wordsworth's "Preface to *Lyrical Ballads*"; Coleridge's introduction to *Biographia Literaria;* Eliot's "Tradition and the Individual Talent"; Empson's *Seven Types of Ambiguity;* and numerous others. And that list has lengthened in the last thirty years. I began to realize, when I started to write this talk, that the present wave of United States feminism has, in a little over ten years, produced some equally indispensable critical texts—which are by extension cultural criticism. If *Sexual Politics*, through its ambitious synthesis and high visibility, opened the way, Barbara Smith's "Toward a Black Feminist Criticism" was the antithetical necessary next step, acknowledging what had been done and driving a critique into the hearts of both white feminist and Black literary criticism. I think, then, of writings—and here I am by no means chronological—such as Mab Segrest's essay "Southern Women Writing: Toward a Literature of Wholeness";[9] of the essays by Jan Clausen and Gloria T. Hull I have quoted here; of Elly Bulkin's introductions to *Lesbian Fiction* and *Lesbian Poetry*. [10] I think of Alice Walker's "In Search of Our Mothers' Gardens" and "One Child of One's Own"; of Gloria Anzaldúa's "Speaking in Tongues: A Letter to Third World Women Writers";[11] of Irena Klepfisz's remarkable story "The Journal of Rachel Robotnik," which *is* lesbian-feminist literary theory in a new form.[12] I would hope that feminist literary critics within the academy feel a responsibility to the questions raised by critics who are also activists in the movement. I wish that academic feminist critics would search out journals like *Azalea, Conditions, Feminary, Sinister Wisdom* and see them for what they are—very tough and subversive historical entities, not all of a piece or pursuing a single "correct line," but calling into

9. [A.R., 1986: Mab Segrest, "Southern Women Writing: Toward a Literature of Wholeness," in *My Mama's Dead Squirrel: Lesbian Essays on Southern Culture* (Ithaca, N.Y.: Firebrand, 1985).]

10. Elly Bulkin, ed., *Lesbian Fiction: An Anthology* (Watertown, Mass.: Persephone, 1981); and Elly Bulkin and Joan Larkin, eds., *Lesbian Poetry* (Watertown, Mass.: Persephone, 1981; distributed by Gay Press, Boston, Massachusetts).

11. Gloria Anzaldúa, "Speaking in Tongues: A Letter to Third World Women Writers," in *This Bridge Called My Back*, ed. Cherríe Moraga and Gloria Anzaldúa (Watertown, Mass.: Persephone, 1981).

12. Irena Klepfisz, "The Journal of Rachel Robotnik," *Conditions* 6 (1980): 1. [A.R., 1986: Reprinted in Irena Klepfisz, *Different Enclosures* (London: Onlywomen, 1985).]

question most of the activity of the dominant lit. crit. and the culture it reflects, and absolutely needed in the classroom. I hope that feminist criticism can renounce the temptation to be graceful, pleasing, and respectable and strive instead to be strong-minded, rash, and dangerous. I hope that feminist critics in the universities can take their own work seriously as a political force, as part of the network of communications for the survival of our movement. I wish for all of us—writers, reviewers, editors, scholars, organizers, booksellers, printers, publishers, students, and teachers—to share in the power of each others' work.

Split at the Root: An Essay on Jewish Identity (1982)

For about fifteen minutes I have been sitting chin in hand in front of the typewriter, staring out at the snow. Trying to be honest with myself, trying to figure out why writing this seems to be so dangerous an act, filled with fear and shame, and why it seems so necessary. It comes to me that in order to write this I have to be willing to do two things: I have to claim my father, for I have my Jewishness from him and not from my gentile mother; and I have to break his silence, his taboos; in order to claim him I have in a sense to expose him.

And there is, of course, the third thing: I have to face the sources and the flickering presence of my own ambivalence as a Jew; the daily, mundane anti-Semitisms of my entire life.

These are stories I have never tried to tell before. Why now? Why, I asked myself sometime last year, does this question of Jewish identity float so impalpably, so ungraspably around me, a cloud I can't quite see the outlines of, which feels to me to be without definition?

I wrote this essay in 1982 for Evelyn Torton Beck's Nice Jewish Girls: A Lesbian Anthology. *It was later reprinted in* Fathers, *an anthology edited by Ursula Owen for Virago Ltd., in London, and published in the United States by Pantheon.*

And yet I've been on the track of this longer than I think.

In a long poem written in 1960, when I was thirty-one years old, I described myself as "Split at the root, neither Gentile nor Jew, / Yankee nor Rebel."[1] I was still trying to have it both ways: to be neither/nor, trying to live (with my Jewish husband and three children more Jewish in ancestry than I) in the predominantly gentile Yankee academic world of Cambridge, Massachusetts.

But this begins, for me, in Baltimore, where I was born in my father's workplace, a hospital in the Black ghetto, whose lobby contained an immense white marble statue of Christ.

My father was then a young teacher and researcher in the department of pathology at the Johns Hopkins Medical School, one of the very few Jews to attend or teach at that institution. He was from Birmingham, Alabama; his father, Samuel, was Ashkenazic, an immigrant from Austria-Hungary and his mother, Hattie Rice, a Sephardic Jew from Vicksburg, Mississippi. My grandfather had had a shoe store in Birmingham, which did well enough to allow him to retire comfortably and to leave my grandmother income on his death. The only souvenirs of my grandfather, Samuel Rich, were his ivory flute, which lay on our living-room mantel and was not to be played with; his thin gold pocket watch, which my father wore; and his Hebrew prayer book, which I discovered among my father's books in the course of reading my way through his library. In this prayer book there was a newspaper clipping about my grandparents' wedding, which took place in a synagogue.

My father, Arnold, was sent in adolescence to a military

---

1. Adrienne Rich, "Readings of History," in *Snapshots of a Daughter-in-Law* (New York: W. W. Norton, 1967), pp. 36–40.

school in the North Carolina mountains, a place for training white southern Christian gentlemen. I suspect that there were few, if any, other Jewish boys at Colonel Bingham's, or at "Mr. Jefferson's university" in Charlottesville, where he studied as an undergraduate. With whatever conscious forethought, Samuel and Hattie sent their son into the dominant southern WASP culture to become an "exception," to enter the professional class. Never, in describing these experiences, did he speak of having suffered—from loneliness, cultural alienation, or outsiderhood. Never did I hear him use the word *anti-Semitism*.

It was only in college, when I read a poem by Karl Shapiro beginning "To hate the Negro and avoid the Jew / is the curriculum," that it flashed on me that there was an untold side to my father's story of his student years. He looked recognizably Jewish, was short and slender in build with dark wiry hair and deep-set eyes, high forehead and curved nose.

My mother is a gentile. In Jewish law I cannot count myself a Jew. If it is true that "we think back through our mothers if we are women" (Virginia Woolf)—and I myself have affirmed this—then even according to lesbian theory, I cannot (or need not?) count myself a Jew.

The white southern Protestant woman, the gentile, has always been there for me to peel back into. That's a whole piece of history in itself, for my gentile grandmother and my mother were also frustrated artists and intellectuals, a lost writer and a lost composer between them. Readers and annotators of books, note takers, my mother a good pianist still, in her eighties. But there was also the obsession with ancestry, with "background," the southern talk of family, not as people you would necessarily know and depend on, but as heritage, the guarantee of "good breeding." There was the inveterate romantic heterosexual fantasy, the mother telling the daughter how to attract men (my mother often used the word "fascinate"); the assumption that relations between the sexes could only be romantic, that it was in the woman's interest to cultivate "mystery," conceal her actual feelings. Survival tactics of a kind, I think today, knowing what I know about the white woman's sexual role in the southern racist scenario. Heterosexuality as protection, but also drawing white women deeper into collusion with white men.

It would be easy to push away and deny the gentile in me —that white southern woman, that social christian. At different times in my life I have wanted to push away one or the other burden of inheritance, to say merely *I am a woman; I am a lesbian.* If I call myself a Jewish lesbian, do I thereby try to shed some of my southern gentile white woman's culpability? If I call myself only through my mother, is it because I pass more easily through a world where being a lesbian often seems like outsiderhood enough?

According to Nazi logic, my two Jewish grandparents would have made me a *Mischling, first-degree*—nonexempt from the Final Solution.

The social world in which I grew up was christian virtually without needing to say so—christian imagery, music, language, symbols, assumptions everywhere. It was also a genteel, white, middle-class world in which "common" was a term of deep opprobrium. "Common" white people might speak of "niggers"; *we* were taught never to use that word—*we* said "Negroes" (even as we accepted segregation, the eating taboo, the assumption that Black people were simply of a separate species). Our language was more polite, distinguishing us from the "red-necks" or the lynch-mob mentality. But so charged with negative meaning was even the word "Negro" that as children we were taught never to use it in front of Black people. We were taught that any mention of skin color in the presence of colored people was treacherous, forbidden ground. In a parallel way, the word "Jew" was not used by polite gentiles. I sometimes heard my best friend's father, a Presbyterian minister, allude to "the Hebrew people" or "people of the Jewish faith." The world of acceptable folk was white, gentile (christian, really), and had "ideals" (which colored people, white "common" people, were not supposed to have). "Ideals" and "manners" included not hurting someone's feelings by calling her or him a Negro or a Jew—naming the hated identity. This is the mental framework of the 1930s and 1940s in which I was raised.

(Writing this, I feel dimly like the betrayer: of my father, who did not speak the word; of my mother, who must have trained me in the messages; of my caste and class; of my whiteness itself.)

Two memories: I am in a play reading at school of *The Merchant of Venice.* Whatever Jewish law says, I am quite sure I was *seen* as Jewish (with a reassuringly gentile mother) in that double vision that bigotry allows. I am the only Jewish girl in the class, and I am playing Portia. As always, I read my part aloud for my father the night before, and he tells me to convey, with my voice, more scorn and contempt with the word "Jew": "Therefore, Jew . . . " I have to say the word out, and say it loudly. I was encouraged to pretend to be a non-Jewish child acting a non-Jewish character who has to speak the word "Jew" emphatically. Such a child would not have had trouble with the part. But *I* must have had trouble with the part, if only because the word itself was really taboo. I can see that there was a kind of terrible, bitter bravado about my father's way of handling this. And who would not dissociate from Shylock in order to identify with Portia? As a Jewish child who was also a female,

I loved Portia—and, like every other Shakespearean heroine, she proved a treacherous role model.

A year or so later I am in another play, *The School for Scandal,* in which a notorious spendthrift is described as having "many excellent friends . . . among the Jews." In neither case was anything explained, either to me or to the class at large, about this scorn for Jews and the disgust surrounding Jews and money. Money, when Jews wanted it, had it, or lent it to others, seemed to take on a peculiar nastiness; Jews and money had some peculiar and unspeakable relation.

At this same school—in which we had Episcopalian hymns and prayers, and read aloud through the Bible morning after morning—I gained the impression that Jews were in the Bible and mentioned in English literature, that they had been persecuted centuries ago by the wicked Inquisition, but that they seemed not to exist in everyday life. These were the 1940s, and we were told a great deal about the Battle of Britain, the noble French Resistance fighters, the brave, starving Dutch—but I did not learn of the resistance of the Warsaw ghetto until I left home.

I was sent to the Episcopal church, baptized and confirmed, and attended it for about five years, though without belief. That religion seemed to have little to do with belief or commitment; it was liturgy that mattered, not spiritual passion. Neither of my parents ever entered that church, and my father would not enter *any* church for any reason—wedding or funeral. Nor did I enter a synagogue until I left Baltimore. When I came home from church, for a while, my father insisted on reading aloud to me from Thomas Paine's *The Age of Reason* —a diatribe against institutional religion. Thus, he explained, I would have a balanced view of these things, a choice. He— they—did not give me the choice to be a Jew. My mother explained to me when I was filling out forms for college that if any question was asked about "religion," I should put down "Episcopalian" rather than "none"—to seem to have no religion was, she implied, dangerous.

But it was white social christianity, rather than any particular christian sect, that the world was founded on. The very word *Christian* was used as a synonym for virtuous, just, peace-loving, generous, etc., etc.[2] The norm was christian: "religion: none" was indeed not acceptable. Anti-Semitism was so intrinsic as not to have a name. I don't recall exactly being taught that the Jews killed Jesus—"Christ killer" seems too strong a term for the bland Episcopal vocabulary—but certainly we got the impression that the Jews had been caught out in a terrible mistake, failing to recognize the true Messiah, and were thereby less advanced in moral and spiritual sensibility. The Jews had actually allowed *moneylenders in the Temple* (again, the unexplained obsession with Jews and money). They were of the past, archaic, primitive, as older (and darker) cultures are supposed to be primitive; christianity was lightness, fairness, peace on earth, and combined the feminine appeal of "The meek shall inherit the earth" with the masculine stride of "Onward, Christian Soldiers."

Sometime in 1946, while still in high school, I read in the newspaper that a theater in Baltimore was showing films of the Allied liberation of the Nazi concentration camps. Alone, I went downtown after school one afternoon and watched the stark, blurry, but unmistakable newsreels. When I try to go back and touch the pulse of that girl of sixteen, growing up in many ways so precocious and so ignorant, I am overwhelmed by a memory of despair, a sense of inevitability more envelop-

2. In a similar way the phrase "That's white of you" implied that you were behaving with the superior decency and morality expected of white but not of Black people.

ing than any I had ever known. Anne Frank's diary and many other personal narratives of the Holocaust were still unknown or unwritten. But it came to me that every one of those piles of corpses, mountains of shoes and clothing had contained, simply, individuals, who had believed, as I now believed of myself, that they were intended to live out a life of some kind of meaning, that the world possessed some kind of sense and order; yet *this* had happened to them. And I, who believed my life was intended to be so interesting and meaningful, was connected to those dead by something—not just mortality but a taboo name, a hated identity. Or was I—did I really have to be? Writing this now, I feel belated rage that I was so impoverished by the family and social worlds I lived in, that I had to try to figure out by myself what this did indeed mean for me. That I had never been taught about resistance, only about passing. That I had no language for anti-Semitism itself.

When I went home and told my parents where I had been, they were not pleased. I felt accused of being morbidly curious, not healthy, sniffing around death for the thrill of it. And since, at sixteen, I was often not sure of the sources of my feelings or of my motives for doing what I did, I probably accused myself as well. One thing was clear: there was nobody in my world with whom I could discuss those films. Probably at the same time, I was reading accounts of the camps in magazines and newspapers; what I remember were the films and having questions that I could not even phrase, such as *Are those men and women "them" or "us"?*

To be able to ask even the child's astonished question *Why do they hate us so?* means knowing how to say "we." The guilt of not knowing, the guilt of perhaps having betrayed my parents or even those victims, those survivors, through mere curiosity—these also froze in me for years the impulse to find out more about the Holocaust.

1947: I left Baltimore to go to college in Cambridge, Massachusetts, left (I thought) the backward, enervating South for the intellectual, vital North. New England also had for me some vibration of higher moral rectitude, of moral passion even, with its seventeenth-century Puritan self-scrutiny, its nineteenth-century literary "flowering," its abolitionist righteousness, Colonel Shaw and his Black Civil War regiment depicted in granite on Boston Common. At the same time, I found myself, at Radcliffe, among Jewish women. I used to sit for hours over coffee with what I thought of as the "real" Jewish students, who told me about middle-class Jewish culture in America. I described my background—for the first time to strangers—and they took me on, some with amusement at my illiteracy, some arguing that I could never marry into a strict Jewish family, some convinced I didn't "look Jewish," others that I did. I learned the names of holidays and foods, which surnames are Jewish and which are "changed names"; about girls who had had their noses "fixed," their hair straightened. For these young Jewish women, students in the late 1940s, it was acceptable, perhaps even necessary, to strive to look as gentile as possible; but they stuck proudly to being Jewish, expected to marry a Jew, have children, keep the holidays, carry on the culture.

I felt I was testing a forbidden current, that there was danger in these revelations. I bought a reproduction of a Chagall portrait of a rabbi in striped prayer shawl and hung it on the wall of my room. I was admittedly young and trying to educate myself, but I was also doing something that *is* dangerous: I was flirting with identity.

One day that year I was in a small shop where I had bought a dress with a too-long skirt. The shop employed a seamstress who did alterations, and she came in to pin up the skirt on me.

I am sure that she was a recent immigrant, a survivor. I remember a short, dark woman wearing heavy glasses, with an accent so foreign I could not understand her words. Something about her presence was very powerful and disturbing to me. After marking and pinning up the skirt, she sat back on her knees, looked up at me, and asked in a hurried whisper: "You Jewish?" Eighteen years of training in assimilation sprang into the reflex by which I shook my head, rejecting her, and muttered, "No."

What was I actually saying "no" to? She was poor, older, struggling with a foreign tongue, anxious; she had escaped the death that had been intended for her, but I had no imagination of her possible courage and foresight, her resistance—I did not see in her a heroine who had perhaps saved many lives, including her own. I saw the frightened immigrant, the seamstress hemming the skirts of college girls, the wandering Jew. But I was an American college girl having her skirt hemmed. And I was frightened myself, I think, because she had recognized me ("It takes one to know one," my friend Edie at Radcliffe had said) even if I refused to recognize myself or her, even if her recognition was sharpened by loneliness or the need to feel safe with me.

But why should she have felt safe with me? I myself was living with a false sense of safety.

There are betrayals in my life that I have known at the very moment were betrayals: this was one of them. There are other betrayals committed so repeatedly, so mundanely, that they leave no memory trace behind, only a growing residue of misery, of dull, accreted self-hatred. Often these take the form not of words but of silence. Silence before the joke at which everyone is laughing: the anti-woman joke, the racist joke, the anti-Semitic joke. Silence and then amnesia. Blocking it out when the oppressor's language starts coming from the lips of one we admire, whose courage and eloquence have touched us: *She didn't really mean that; he didn't really say that.* But the accretions build up out of sight, like scale inside a kettle.

1948: I come home from my freshman year at college, flaming with new insights, new information. I am the daughter who has gone out into the world, to the pinnacle of intellectual prestige, Harvard, fulfilling my father's hopes for me, but also exposed to dangerous influences. I have already been reproved for attending a rally for Henry Wallace and the Progressive party. I challenge my father: "Why haven't you told me that I am Jewish? Why do you never talk about being a Jew?" He answers measuredly, "You know that I have never denied that I am a Jew. But it's not important to me. I am a scientist, a deist. I have no use for organized religion. I choose to live in a world of many kinds of people. There are Jews I admire and others whom I despise. I am a person, not simply a Jew." The words are as I remember them, not perhaps exactly as spoken. But that was the message. And it contained enough truth—as all denial drugs itself on partial truth—so that it remained for the time being unanswerable, leaving me high and dry, split at the root, gasping for clarity, for air.

At that time Arnold Rich was living in suspension, waiting to be appointed to the professorship of pathology at Johns Hopkins. The appointment was delayed for years, no Jew ever having held a professional chair in that medical school. And he wanted it badly. It must have been a very bitter time for him, since he had believed so greatly in the redeeming power of excellence, of being the most brilliant, inspired man for the job. With enough excellence, you could presumably make it stop mattering that you were Jewish; you could become the *only* Jew in the gentile world, a Jew so "civilized," so far from "common," so attractively combining southern gentility with European cultural values that no one would ever confuse you with the raw, "pushy" Jews of New York, the "loud, hysterical" refugees from eastern Europe, the "overdressed" Jews of the urban South.

We—my sister, mother, and I—were constantly urged to speak quietly in public, to dress without ostentation, to repress all vividness or spontaneity, to assimilate with a world which might see us as too flamboyant. I suppose that my mother, pure gentile though she was, could be seen as acting "common" or "Jewish" if she laughed too loudly or spoke aggressively. My father's mother, who lived with us half the year, was a model of circumspect behavior, dressed in dark blue or lavender, retiring in company, ladylike to an extreme, wearing no jewelry except a good gold chain, a narrow brooch, or a string of pearls. A few times, within the family, I saw her anger flare, felt the passion she was repressing. But when Arnold took us out to a restaurant or on a trip, the Rich women were always tuned down to some WASP level my father believed, surely, would protect us all—maybe also make us unrecognizable to the "real Jews" who wanted to seize us, drag us back to the *shtetl*, the ghetto, in its many manifestations.

For, yes, that *was* a message—that some Jews would be after you, once they "knew," to rejoin them, to re-enter a world that was messy, noisy, unpredictable, maybe poor—"even though," as my mother once wrote me, criticizing my largely Jewish choice of friends in college, "some of them will be the most brilliant, fascinating people you'll ever meet." I wonder if that isn't one message of assimilation—of America—that the unlucky or the unachieving want to pull you backward, that to identify with them is to court downward mobility, lose the precious chance of passing, of token existence. There was always within this sense of Jewish identity a strong class discrimination. Jews might be "fascinating" as individuals but came with huge unruly families who "poured chicken soup over everyone's head" (in the phrase of a white southern male poet). Anti-Semitism could thus be justified by the bad behavior of certain Jews; and if you did not effectively deny family and community, there would always be a remote cousin claiming kinship with you who was the "wrong kind" of Jew.

I have always believed his attitude toward other Jews depended on who they were. . . . It was my impression that Jews of this background looked down on Eastern European Jews, including Polish Jews and Russian Jews, who generally were not as well educated. This from a letter written to me recently by a gentile who had worked in my father's department, whom I had asked about anti-Semitism there and in particular regarding my father. This informant also wrote me that it was hard to perceive anti-Semitism in Baltimore because the racism made so much more intense an impression: *I would almost have to think that blacks went to a different heaven than the whites, because the bodies were kept in a separate morgue, and some white persons did not even want blood transfusions from black donors.* My father's mind was predictably racist and misogynist; yet as a medical student he noted in his journal that southern male chivalry stopped at the point of any white man in a streetcar giving his seat to an old, weary Black woman standing in the aisle. Was this a Jewish insight—an outsider's insight, even though the outsider was striving to be on the inside?

Because what isn't named is often more permeating than what is, I believe that my father's Jewishness profoundly shaped my own identity and our family existence. They were shaped both by external anti-Semitism and my father's self-hatred, and by his Jewish pride. What Arnold did, I think, was call his Jewish pride something else: achievement, aspiration, genius, idealism. Whatever was unacceptable got left back under the rubric of Jewishness or the "wrong kind" of Jews—

uneducated, aggressive, loud. The message I got was that we were really superior: nobody else's father had collected so many books, had traveled so far, knew so many languages. Baltimore was a musical city, but for the most part, in the families of my school friends, culture was for women. My father was an amateur musician, read poetry, adored encyclopedic knowledge. He prowled and pounced over my school papers, insisting I use "grown-up" sources; he criticized my poems for faulty technique and gave me books on rhyme and meter and form. His investment in my intellect and talent was egotistical, tyrannical, opinionated, and terribly wearing. He taught me, nevertheless, to believe in hard work, to mistrust easy inspiration, to write and rewrite; to feel that I *was* a person of the book, even though a woman; to take ideas seriously. He made me feel, at a very young age, the power of language and that I could share in it.

The Riches were proud, but we also had to be very careful. Our behavior had to be more impeccable than other people's. Strangers were not to be trusted, nor even friends; family issues must never go beyond the family; the world was full of potential slanderers, betrayers, *people who could not understand.* Even within the family, I realize that I never in my whole life knew what my father was really feeling. Yet he spoke— monologued—with driving intensity. You could grow up in such a house mesmerized by the local electricity, the crucial meanings assumed by the merest things. This used to seem to me a sign that we were all living on some high emotional plane. It was a difficult force field for a favored daughter to disengage from.

Easy to call that intensity Jewish; and I have no doubt that passion is one of the qualities required for survival over generations of persecution. But what happens when passion is rent from its original base, when the white gentile world is softly

saying "Be more like us and you can be almost one of us"?
What happens when survival seems to mean closing off one
emotional artery after another? His forebears in Europe had
been forbidden to travel or expelled from one country after
another, had special taxes levied on them if they left the city
walls, had been forced to wear special clothes and badges,
restricted to the poorest neighborhoods. He had wanted to be
a "free spirit," to travel widely, among "all kinds of people."
Yet in his prime of life he lived in an increasingly withdrawn
world, in his house up on a hill in a neighborhood where Jews
were not supposed to be able to buy property, depending al-
most exclusively on interactions with his wife and daughters to
provide emotional connectedness. In his home, he created a
private defense system so elaborate that even as he was dying,
my mother felt unable to talk freely with his colleagues or
others who might have helped her. Of course, she acquiesced
in this.

The loneliness of the "only," the token, often doesn't feel
like loneliness but like a kind of dead echo chamber. Certain
things that ought to don't resonate. Somewhere Beverly Smith
writes of women of color "inspiring the behavior" in each
other. When there's nobody to "inspire the behavior," act out
of the culture, there is an atrophy, a dwindling, which is partly
invisible.

I was married in 1953, in the Hillel House at Harvard, under
a portrait of Albert Einstein. My parents refused to come. I was
marrying a Jew of the "wrong kind" from an Orthodox eastern
European background. Brooklyn-born, he had gone to Har-
vard, changed his name, was both indissolubly connected to his
childhood world and terribly ambivalent about it. My father
saw this marriage as my having fallen prey to the Jewish family,
eastern European division.

Like many women I knew in the fifties living under a then-unquestioned heterosexual imperative, I married in part because I knew no better way to disconnect from my first family. I married a "real Jew" who was himself almost equally divided between a troubled yet ingrained Jewish identity, and the pull toward Yankee approval, assimilation. But at least he was not adrift as a single token in a gentile world. We lived in a world where there was much intermarriage and where a certain "Jewish flavor" was accepted within the dominant gentile culture. People talked glibly of "Jewish self-hatred," but anti-Semitism was rarely identified. It was as if you could have it both ways —identity and assimilation—without having to think about it very much.

I was moved and gratefully amazed by the affection and kindliness my husband's parents showed me, the half *shiksa.* I longed to embrace that family, that new and mysterious Jewish world. It was never a question of conversion—my husband had long since ceased being observant—but of a burning desire to do well, please these new parents, heal the split consciousness in which I had been raised, and, of course, to belong. In the big, sunny apartment on Eastern Parkway, the table would be spread on Saturday afternoons with a white or an embroidered cloth and plates of coffeecake, spongecake, mohncake, cookies for a family gathering where everyone ate and drank—coffee, milk, cake—and later the talk still eddied among the women around the table or in the kitchen, while the men ended up in the living room watching the ball game. I had never known this kind of family, in which mock insults were cheerfully exchanged, secrets whispered in corners among two or three, children and grandchildren boasted about, and the new daughter-in-law openly inspected. I was profoundly attracted by all this, including the punctilious observance of *kashrut,* the symbolism lurking behind daily kitchen tasks. I saw it all as quintes-

sentially and authentically Jewish, and I objectified both the
people and the culture. My unexamined anti-Semitism allowed
me to do this. But also, I had not yet recognized that as a
woman I stood in a particular and unexamined relationship to
the Jewish family and to Jewish culture.

There were several years during which I did not see, and
barely communicated with, my parents. At the same time, my
father's personality haunted my life. Such had been the force
of his will in our household that for a long time I felt I would
have to pay in some terrible way for having disobeyed him.
When finally we were reconciled, and my husband and I and
our children began to have some minimal formal contact with
my parents, the obsessional power of Arnold's voice or hand-
writing had given way to a dull sense of useless anger and pain.
I wanted him to cherish and approve of me, not as he had when
I was a child, but as the woman I was, who had her own mind
and had made her own choices. This, I finally realized, was not
to be; Arnold demanded absolute loyalty, absolute submission
to his will. In my separation from him, in my realization at
what price that once-intoxicating approval had been bought, I
was learning in concrete ways a great deal about patriarchy, in
particular how the "special" woman, the favored daughter, is
controlled and rewarded.

Arnold Rich died in 1968 after a long, deteriorating illness;
his mind had gone, and he had been losing his sight for years.
It was a year of intensifying political awareness for me: the
Martin Luther King and Robert Kennedy assassinations, the
Columbia strike. But it was not that these events, and the
meetings and demonstrations that surrounded them, pre-
empted the time of mourning for my father; I had been mourn-
ing a long time for an early, primary, and intense relationship,
by no means always benign, but in which I had been ceaselessly
made to feel that what I did with my life, the choices I made,
the attitudes I held, were of the utmost consequence.

Sometime in my thirties, on visits to Brooklyn, I sat on Eastern Parkway, a baby stroller at my feet—one of many rows of young Jewish women on benches with children in that neighborhood. I used to see the Lubavitcher Hasidim—then beginning to move into the Crown Heights neighborhood—walking out on *Shabbes*, the women in their *shaytls* a little behind the men. My father-in-law pointed them out as rather exotic—too old-country, perhaps, too unassimilated even for his devout yet Americanized sense of Jewish identity. It took many years for me to understand—partly because I understood so little about class in America—how in my own family, and in the very different family of my in-laws, there were degrees and hierarchies of assimilation which looked askance upon each other—and also geographic lines of difference, as between southern Jews and New York Jews, whose manners and customs varied along class as well as regional lines.

I had three sons before I was thirty, and during those years I often felt that to be a Jewish woman, a Jewish mother, was to be perceived in the Jewish family as an entirely physical being, a producer and nourisher of children. The experience of motherhood was eventually to radicalize me. But before that, I was encountering the institution of motherhood most directly in a Jewish cultural version; and I felt rebellious, moody, defensive, unable to sort out what was Jewish from what was simply motherhood or female destiny. (I lived in Cambridge, not Brooklyn; but there, too, restless, educated women sat on benches with baby strollers, half-stunned, not by Jewish cultural expectations, but by the middle-class American social expectations of the 1950s.)

My children were taken irregularly to Seders, to bar mizvahs, and to special services in their grandfather's temple. Their father lit Hanukkah candles while I stood by, having rememorized each year the English meaning of the Hebrew blessing.

We all celebrated a secular, liberal Christmas. I read aloud from books about Esther and the Maccabees and Moses, and also from books about Norse trolls and Chinese grandmothers and Celtic dragon slayers. Their father told stories of his boyhood in Brooklyn, his grandmother in the Bronx who had to be visited by subway every week, of misdeeds in Hebrew school, of being a bright Jewish kid at Boys' High. In the permissive liberalism of academic Cambridge, you could raise your children to be as vaguely or distinctly Jewish as you would, but Christian myth and calendar organized the year. My sons grew up knowing far more about the existence and concrete meaning of Jewish culture than I had. But I don't recall sitting down with them and telling them that millions of people like themselves, many of them children, had been rounded up and murdered in Europe in their parents' lifetime. Nor was I able to tell them that they came in part out of the rich, thousand-year-old Ashkenazic culture of eastern Europe, which the Holocaust destroyed; or that they came from a people whose traditions, religious and secular, included a hatred of oppression and an imperative to pursue justice and care for the stranger—an anti-racist, a socialist, and even sometimes a feminist vision. I could not tell them these things because these things were still too indistinct in my own mind.

The emergence of the Civil Rights movement in the sixties I remember as lifting me out of a sense of personal frustration and hopelessness. Reading James Baldwin's early essays in the fifties had stirred me with a sense that apparently "given" situations like racism could be analyzed and described and that this could lead to action, to change. Racism had been so utter and implicit a fact of my childhood and adolescence, had felt so central among the silences, negations, cruelties, fears, superstitions of my early life, that somewhere among my feelings must have been the hope that if Black people could become free of the immense political and social burdens they were forced to bear, I, too, could become free of all the ghosts and shadows of my childhood, named and unnamed. When "the movement" began, it felt extremely personal to me. And it was often Jews who spoke up for the justice of the cause, Jewish students and civil rights lawyers who travelled South; it was two young Jews who were found murdered with a young Black man in Mississippi: Schwerner, Goodman, Chaney.

Moving to New York in the mid-sixties meant being plunged almost immediately into the debate over community control of public schools, in which Black and Jewish teachers and parents were often on opposite sides of extremely militant barricades. It was easy as a white liberal to deplore and condemn the racism of middle-class Jewish parents or angry Jewish school-teachers, many of them older women; to displace our own racism onto them; or to feel it as too painful to think about. The struggle for Black civil rights had such clarity about it for me: I knew that segregation was wrong, that unequal opportunity was wrong; I knew that segregation in particular was more than a set of social and legal rules—it meant that even "decent" white people lived in a network of lies and arrogance and moral collusion. In the world of Jewish assimilationist and liberal politics which I knew best, however, things were far less clear to me, and anti-Semitism went almost unmentioned. It was even possible to view concern about anti-Semitism as a reactionary agenda, a monomania of *Commentary* magazine or, later, the Jewish Defense League. Most of the political work I was doing in the late 1960s was on racial issues, in particular as a teacher in the City University during the struggle for open admissions. The white colleagues I thought of as allies were, I think, mostly Jewish. Yet it was easy to see other New York

Jews, who had climbed out of poverty and exploitation through the public-school system and the free city colleges, as now trying to block Black and Puerto Rican students trying to do likewise. I didn't understand then that I was living between two strains of Jewish social identity: the Jew as radical visionary and activist who understands oppression firsthand, and the Jew as part of America's devouring plan in which the persecuted, called to assimilation, learn that the price is to engage in persecution.

And, indeed, there *was* intense racism among Jews as well as white gentiles in the City University, part of the bitter history of Jews and Blacks which James Baldwin had described much earlier, in his 1948 essay "The Harlem Ghetto";[3] part of the divide-and-conquer script still being rehearsed by those of us who have the least to gain from it.

By the time I left my marriage, after seventeen years and three children, I had become identified with the Women's Liberation movement. It was an astonishing time to be a woman of my age. In the 1950s, seeking a way to grasp the pain I seemed to be feeling most of the time, to set it in some larger context, I had read all kinds of things; but it was James Baldwin and Simone de Beauvoir who had described the world—though differently—in terms that made the most sense to me. By the end of the sixties there were two political movements—one already meeting severe repression, one just emerging—which addressed those descriptions of the world.

And there was, of course, a third movement, or a movement-within-a-movement: the early lesbian manifestoes, the new visibility and activism of lesbians everywhere. I had known very

---

3. James Baldwin, "The Harlem Ghetto," in *Notes of a Native Son* (Boston: Beacon, 1955).

early on that the women's movement was not going to be a simple walk across an open field; that it would pull on every fiber of my existence; that it would mean going back and searching the shadows of my consciousness. Reading *The Second Sex* in the 1950s isolation of an academic housewife had felt less dangerous than reading "The Myth of Vaginal Orgasm" or "Woman-identified Woman" in a world where I was in constant debate and discussion with women over every aspect of our lives that we could as yet name. De Beauvoir had placed "The Lesbian" on the margins, and there was little in her book to suggest the power of woman bonding. But the passion of debating ideas with women was an erotic passion for me, and the risking of self with women that was necessary in order to win some truth out of the lies of the past was also erotic. The suppressed lesbian I had been carrying in me since adolescence began to stretch her limbs, and her first full-fledged act was to fall in love with a Jewish woman.

Some time during the early months of that relationship, I dreamed that I was arguing feminist politics with my lover. *Of course,* I said to her in this dream, *if you're going to bring up the Holocaust against me, there's nothing I can do.* If, as I believe, I was both myself and her in this dream, it spoke of the split in my consciousness. I had been, more or less, a Jewish heterosexual woman. But what did it mean to be a Jewish lesbian? What did it mean to feel myself, as I did, both anti-Semite and Jew? And, as a feminist, how was I charting for myself the oppressions within oppression?

The earliest feminist papers on Jewish identity that I read were critiques of the patriarchal and misogynist elements in Judaism, or of the caricaturing of Jewish women in literature by Jewish men. I remember hearing Judith Plaskow give a paper called "Can a Woman Be a Jew?" (Her conclusion was "Yes, but . . . ") I was soon after in correspondence with a former student who had emigrated to Israel, was a passionate feminist, and wrote to me at length of the legal and social constraints on women there, the stirrings of contemporary Israeli feminism, and the contradictions she felt in her daily life. With the new politics, activism, literature of a tumultuous feminist movement around me, a movement which claimed universality though it had not yet acknowledged its own racial, class, and ethnic perspectives or its fears of the differences among women, I pushed aside for one last time thinking further about myself as a Jewish woman. I saw Judaism simply as another strand of patriarchy. If asked to choose, I might have said (as my father had said in other language): *I am a woman, not a Jew.* (But, I always added mentally, if Jews had to wear yellow stars again, I, too, would wear one—as if I would have the choice to wear it or not.)

Sometimes I feel I have seen too long from too many disconnected angles: white, Jewish, anti-Semite, racist, anti-racist, once-married, lesbian, middle-class, feminist, exmatriate southerner, *split at the root*—that I will never bring them whole. I would have liked, in this essay, to bring together the meanings of anti-Semitism and racism as I have experienced them and as I believe they intersect in the world beyond my life. But I'm not able to do this yet. I feel the tension as I think, make notes: *If you really look at the one reality, the other will waver and disperse.* Trying in one week to read Angela Davis and Lucy Davidowicz;[4] trying to hold throughout to a feminist, a lesbian, perspective—what does this mean? Nothing has trained me for this. And sometimes I feel inadequate to make any statement as a Jew; I feel the history of denial within me like an injury,

4. Angela Y. Davis, *Women, Race and Class* (New York: Random House, 1981); Lucy S. Davidowicz, *The War against the Jews 1933–1945* (1975) (New York: Bantam, 1979).

a scar. For assimilation has affected *my* perceptions; those early lapses in meaning, those blanks, are with me still. My ignorance can be dangerous to me and to others.

Yet we can't wait for the undamaged to make our connections for us; we can't wait to speak until we are perfectly clear and righteous. There is no purity and, in our lifetimes, no end to this process.

This essay, then, has no conclusions: it is another beginning for me. Not just a way of saying, in 1982 Right Wing America, *I, too, will wear the yellow star.* It's a moving into accountability, enlarging the range of accountability. I know that in the rest of my life, the next half century or so, every aspect of my identity will have to be engaged. The middle-class white girl taught to trade obedience for privilege. The Jewish lesbian raised to be a heterosexual gentile. The woman who first heard oppression named and analyzed in the Black Civil Rights struggle. The woman with three sons, the feminist who hates male violence. The woman limping with a cane, the woman who has stopped bleeding are also accountable. The poet who knows that beautiful language can lie, that the oppressor's language sometimes sounds beautiful. The woman trying, as part of her resistance, to clean up her act.

The Eye of the Outsider: Elizabeth Bishop's *Complete Poems, 1927–1979* (1983)

I knew Elizabeth Bishop's poetry very well before I ever met her, and I always knew the poems better than the woman. I had early been drawn to the timbre of the voice in her first two books, had met her once or twice in literary groups, not the best place for breaking through shyness and differences in age and reputation. Much later, in the early 1970s, I offered her a ride from New York to Boston, where we were both then living. We found ourselves talking of the recent suicides in each of our lives, telling "how it happened" as people speak who feel they will be understood. In the course of this drive I forgot to take the turnoff at Hartford, and drove as far as Springfield without noticing. This conversation was the only one approaching intimacy I ever had with Elizabeth Bishop and almost the only time I saw her alone.

I had felt drawn, but also repelled, by Bishop's early work— I mean *repel* in the sense of refusing access, seeming to push away. In part, my difficulties with her were difficulties in the poetry, of Bishop as a young poet finding her own level and her own language. But in part they were difficulties I brought with

Originally published in the Boston Review *(April 1983): 15–17.*

me, as a still younger woman poet already beginning to question sexual identity, looking for a female genealogy, still not yet consciously lesbian. I had not then connected the themes of outsiderhood and marginality in her work, as well as its encodings and obscurities, with a lesbian identity. I was looking for a clear female tradition; the tradition I was discovering was diffuse, elusive, often cryptic. Yet, especially given the times and customs of the 1940s and 1950s, Bishop's work now seems to me remarkably honest and courageous.

Women poets searching for older contemporaries in that period were supposed to look to "Miss" Marianne Moore as the paradigm of what a woman poet might accomplish, and, after her, to "Miss" Bishop. Both had been selected and certified by the literary establishment, which was, as now, white, male, and at least ostensibly heterosexual. Elizabeth Bishop's name was spoken, her books reviewed with deep respect. But attention was paid to her triumphs, her perfections, not to her struggles for self-definition and her sense of difference. In this way, her reputation made her less, rather than more, available to me. The infrequency of her public appearances and her geographic remoteness—living for many years in Brazil, with a woman as it happened, but we didn't know that—made her an indistinct and a problematic life model for a woman poet.

Some of the poems in her first book, *North and South* (1946), I found impenetrable: intellectualized to the point of obliquity (e.g., "The Map"), or using extended metaphor to create a mask (e.g., "A Miracle for Breakfast," "The Monument," "The Imaginary Iceberg"). That first book contains traces of Miss Moore—for example, the coy use of quoted phrases within a poem, a mannerism Bishop soon discarded. And the overall strategy of many poems—the poem-about-an-artifact which becomes the poem-as-artifact—owes too much to Moore. Bishop wrote such poems later in her life (see "12 o'Clock News," for example), but not often. More and more, her poems embodied a need to place herself in the actual, to come to terms with a personal past, with family and class and race, with her presence as a poet in cities and landscapes where human suffering is not a metaphor.

I have been fascinated by the diversity of challenges that *The Complete Poems, 1927–1979* [New York: Farrar, Straus & Giroux, 1983] raises, the questions—poetic and political—that it stirs up, the opportunities that it affords. In addition to the four volumes published in her lifetime, this edition—enhanced by the work of the gifted designer Cynthia Krupat—includes late poems which appeared in magazines after *Geography III* (1976), some posthumously published late poems, eleven poems written between the ages of sixteen and twenty-two, some uncollected later poems, and translations. Part of the value of such a collection is the chance it gives to see where certain obsessions and motives begin to take hold and how they work their way through a lifetime of poems; how certain echoes sound and die away; how style metamorphoses over time. This collection offers not just challenges and questions, but very deep pleasure. In her later work especially, Bishop is difficult to quote from because her poems are so often hung on one long thread; the progression of language and images does not readily separate into extracts. By the same token she is a wonderful poet to read aloud.

Criticism of Bishop in her lifetime was mostly appreciative of her powers of observation, her carefully articulated descriptive language, her wit, her intelligence, the individuality of her voice. I want to acknowledge the distinction of all these, the marvelous flexibility and sturdiness of her writing, her lack of self-indulgence, her capacity to write of loss and of time past without pathos and with precision, as in poems like "Sestina," "The Moose," "Filling Station," "First Death in Nova

Scotia," "At the Fishhouses." I want to pay this homage and go on to aspects of her work which I have not yet seen discussed. In particular I am concerned with her experience of outsiderhood, closely—though not exclusively—linked with the essential outsiderhood of a lesbian identity; and with how the outsider's eye enables Bishop to perceive other kinds of outsiders and to identify, or try to identify, with them. I believe she deserves to be read and valued not only for her language and images or for her personality within the poems, but for the way she locates herself in the world.

Elizabeth Bishop was born in Worcester, Massachusetts, in 1911, and lost her mother into a mental institution when she was five years old—a loss that was permanent. Her father was already dead. She migrated not once, but several times: first to Nova Scotia to be raised by relatives, then back to the United States, then to Brazil, then back to New England after the death of Lota de Soares. Travel—not as in "vacation," not as in "escape"—was from early on a given for her.

> "Continent, city, country, society:
> the choice is never wide and never free,
> And here, or there. . . . No. Should we have stayed at home,
> Wherever that may be?
>   ("Questions of Travel")

The child made "different" because parentless, the emigrant who thinks she would—understandably—"rather have the iceberg than the ship," the woman writing, consciously or not, "against the male flood" (Woolf's phrase), the lesbian writing under the false universal of heterosexuality, the foreigner who can take little for granted—all inhabit Bishop's poetic voice and eye. Outsiderhood is a condition which most people spend (and are often constrained to spend) great energy trying to

deny or evade, through whatever kinds of assimilation or pro-
tective coloration they can manage. Poetry, too, can serve as
protective coloration; the social person who is the poet may also
try to "pass," but the price of external assimilation is internal
division.

The pain of division is acutely present in some of Bishop's
earliest poems, notably in "A Word with You," written when
she was twenty-two, a tense, panicky, one-sided conversation
during which a whole menagerie gets out of control:

> Look out! there's that damned ape again
> sit silently until he goes
> or else forgets the things he knows
> (whatever they are) about us, then
> we can begin to talk again.

In *North and South*, "The Weed" grows up through and
divides the "frozen" heart so that it gushes two "rushing,
half-clear streams." "The Gentleman of Shalott" is a half man
whose other half is actually a reflection in a mirror. "The
Colder the Air" and "Chemin de Fer" can be read as two
bleakly counterpoised possibilities. The "huntress of the winter
air" has everything under control, having reduced the world to
her shooting gallery, in an icy single-mindedness; the speaker
of the poem does not have such power, and beneath its frigid
surface the poem quivers with barely suppressed rage. In "Che-
min de Fer" the speaker is in an endangered position also,
"Alone on the railroad track," while the "dirty hermit" firing
his gun hits nothing, is impotent to carry through:

> "Love should be put into action!"
>   screamed the dirty hermit.
> Across the pond an echo
>   tried and tried to confirm it.

What does it mean to put love into action? Especially in isolation and in a world which does not confirm that imperative?

To know yourself as an outsider, as an "invert" in the old jargon, and to try to live and love in two worlds, is to dream of the impossible safe place, the upside-down park and fountain of "Sleeping on the Ceiling" or, in "Insomnia,"

> that world inverted
> where left is always right
> where the shadows are really the body
> where we stay awake all night,
> where the heavens are shallow as the sea
> is now deep, and you love me.

Or, in "O Breath"—one of a sequence of four short, tensely packed love poems—there is the still ambivalent evocation of

> something that maybe I   could bargain with
> and make a separate peace   beneath
> within   if never with

There is disturbance and tension in these "Four Poems," but there is also a glimpse, at least, of some kind of erotic freeing-up:

> The face is pale
> that tried the puzzle of their prison
> and solved it with an unexpected kiss,
> whose freckled unsuspected hands alit.

The first and title poem of *A Cold Spring* can be read as a record of a slow, deliberate, erotic unfolding, with a culminating image of "shadowy pastures" from which fireflies rise "exactly like the bubbles in champagne." The final poem of this collection, "Shampoo," celebrates a serious, tender, practical rite between two women:

> The shooting stars in your black hair
> in bright formation
> are flocking where,
> so straight, so soon?
> —come, let me wash it in this big tin basin
> battered and shiny like the moon.

But Bishop left behind, in the last unpublished poem of the last year of her life, her own last word on division, decision, and questions of travel:

> Caught—the bubble
> in the spirit-level,
> a creature divided,
> and the compass needle
> wobbling and wavering,
> undecided.
> Freed—the broken
> thermometer's mercury
> running away;
> and the rainbow bird
> from the narrow bevel
> of the empty mirror,
> flying wherever
> it feels like, gay!
>   ("Sonnet")

Poems examining intimate relationship are almost wholly absent from Bishop's later work. What takes their place is a series of poems examining relationships between people who are, for reasons of inequality, distanced: rich and poor, land-

owner and tenant, white woman and Black woman, invader
and native. Even in her first book she had taken on the theme
of the Black woman's existence in a white world. The poem
"Cootchie" addresses the fate of a Black woman who has died,
presumably by drowning, perhaps by suicide. The white
woman she has worked for is literally deaf but also self-
absorbed: she will not "understand." "Songs for a Colored
Singer," rumored to have been written with Billie Holiday in
mind, begins:

> A washing hangs upon the line
> but it's not mine.
> None of the things that I can see
> belong to me . . .

This is a white woman's attempt—respectful, I believe—to
speak through a Black woman's voice. A risky undertaking, and
it betrays the failures and clumsiness of such a position. The
personae we adopt, the degree to which we use lives already
ripped off and violated by our own culture, the problem of
racist stereotyping in every white head, the issue of the writer's
power, right, obligation to speak for others denied a voice, or
the writer's duty to shut up at times or at least to make room
for those who can speak with more immediate authority—
these are crucial questions for our time, and questions that are
relevant to much of Bishop's work. What I value is her attempt
to acknowledge other outsiders, lives marginal in ways that hers
is not, long before the Civil Rights movement made such
awareness temporarily fashionable for some white writers.

Brazil, a multiracial yet still racist and class-fragmented
country, clearly opened up a further range of understanding for
Bishop. Her earliest poems about Brazil grasp the presence of
colonization and enslavement:

Just so the Christians, hard as nails . . .
in creaking armor, came and found it all,
not unfamiliar. . . .
Directly after Mass . . .
they ripped away into the hanging fabric,
each out to catch an Indian for himself—
those maddening little women who kept calling,
calling to each other (or had the birds waked up?)
and retreating, always retreating, behind it.

("Brazil, January 1, 1502")

Some of Bishop's best Brazilian poems are exercises in coming
to terms with her location as a foreign white woman living as
part of a privileged class in a city of beggars and rich people.
I am thinking of "Faustina," "Manuelzinho," "The Burglar of
Babylon," "Pink Dog." In "Faustina" she draws the scene of
a white woman dying in her "crazy house," with her white hair,
among "white disordered sheets," in a white "chamber of
bleached flags," tended by a Black woman servant. The narra-
tor is confronted by the "conundrum" of white power, the
history of what whites have done to Black people, and the
vulnerability of this particular dying old woman. It is a poem
of contradictions and about extremes of possibility between the
two women: a dream of "freedom at last, a lifelong / . . . dream
of protection and rest" versus the "unimaginable nightmare /
that never before dared last / more than a second." Extremes
defined from a white woman's perspective, but at least *ac-
knowledging* the "acuteness of the question." I cannot think
of another poem by a white woman, until some feminist poetry
of the last few years, in which the servant-mistress dynamic
between Black and white women has received unsentimental
attention.[1]

1. It's worth noting that Bishop, clearly selective toward her own work, chose not
to include the poem "A Norther—Key West" in her canon. In this poem, dated 1962,

Bishop precedes "Manuelzinho" with the note "A friend of the writer is speaking," as if partly to dissociate herself from the speaker, a liberal landowner addressing a squatter-tenant. Manuelzinho, the tenant, is seen as improvident, touching, exasperating, picturesque—qualities traditionally attributed to the colonized; the landowner is essentially benign, ruefully resigned to the balance of power in which Manuelzinho must cajole and beg for handouts. In this poem, Bishop places herself between, but not equidistant from, landowner and tenant. There is no way for her to be equidistant: the poem reads, after all, from the landowner's point of view, even though it also exposes her or him. The poem explores that perspective, leaving the reader free to accept or reject it. By contrast, we live through much of "The Burglar of Babylon" in the Burglar's skin; and it's clear that despite the poem's deadpan tone, we are not invited to stay neutral: Micuçu, three times escaped from jail, with a vague array of charges against him, is ambushed by the militia and shot. Soon after his death the soldiers are out on the hills again, searching for two more "enemies of society." The police overkill is ridiculous, the drama recounted in flat-voiced meters. No heroes to this ballad, only victims. Burglars are caught and killed; the essential state of things remains the same:

> On the fair green hills of Rio
> There grows a fearful stain:

---

the observer is distanced and her perceptions distorted by an artificial and brittle tone, betraying an attempted and impossible objectivity. Nor did she include "House Guest" (pre-1969), in which the depressed live-in seamstress is surveyed much as Manuelzinho is—from a "liberal" middle-class perspective. Here, though the poet has evoked a certain tone in which domestic employers have forever discussed employees—frustrated, half-guilty, uncomprehending—she has not found a way to critique the tone and break through the inevitable stereotyping of the seamstress. I am, however, grateful to be able to read these poems and see something of the process of Bishop's own self-criticism and explorations into difficult territory.

> The poor who come to Rio
> And can't go home again. . . .
>
> There's the hill of Kerosene,
>   And the hill of the Skeleton,
> The hill of Astonishment,
>   And the hill of Babylon.

Finally, there is the 1979 poem "Pink Dog," subtitled in brackets "Rio de Janeiro"—a brilliantly bitter, indignant satire on the notion that the wretched of the earth are themselves to blame for their misery and should try to disguise themselves (or assimilate) for their own survival. The hairless female dog with scabies is advised to dress up in a carnival costume and dance the samba:

> (A nursing mother, by those hanging teats.)
> In what slum have you hidden them, poor bitch,
> while you go begging, living by your wits? . . .
>
> If they do this to anyone who begs,
> drugged, drunk, or sober, with or without legs,
> what would they do to sick, four-leggèd dogs?

In selecting the poems I have discussed here, in limited space, I have reluctantly neglected the marvelous Nova Scotia poems as well as many others even better known, such as "Roosters," "The Fish," "Visits to St. Elizabeths" (also a seriously political poem), "In the Waiting Room," "One Art." But it seems to me that Bishop's value for us is more complex and multifaceted than we may have been aware, and I have wanted to suggest new ways of entering her work. Moreover, it is only now, with a decade of feminist and lesbian poetry and criticism behind us and with the publication of these *Complete Poems,* that we can read her as part of a female and lesbian tradition rather than simply as one of the few and "exceptional" women admitted to the male canon. Too often, the "exceptional" or token outsider is praised for her skill and artistry while her deep and troubled connections with other outsiders are ignored. (This is itself part of the imperative to be assimilated.) It is important to me to know that, through most of her life, Bishop was critically and consciously trying to explore marginality, power and powerlessness, often in poetry of great beauty and sensuousness. That not all these poems are fully realized or satisfying simply means that the living who care that art should embody these questions have still more work to do.

Resisting Amnesia: History and Personal Life (1983)

This lecture is dedicated to Joan Kelly, feminist historian, who held the Clark Lectureship here in 1979 and whose untimely death in 1982 was a serious loss to feminists and to feminist history and theory. I want to say her name here and allude to her work, not only because of her thinking, which was passionate, learned, and lucid, and not only because of the personal support she gave me along with so many other feminist writers, activists, teachers, students. She remains a compelling and inspiring figure in part because her understanding of both feminism and history was grounded in her own history as a New York City fireman's daughter who had taken her college degree in night school. She never lost her identification with those who, because of sex, race, or class, have been written off, their lives obscured or distorted, in the texts of white, male, Western historical tradition.

February is Black History Month, and today—February 15 —is the birthday of Susan B. Anthony, a nineteenth-century white woman radical, an anti-slavery activist, a passionate war-

Written for the Clark Lecture, Scripps College, Claremont, California, February 15, 1983.

rior for women's rights, a woman who nonetheless, and to our continuing disadvantage, was finally unable to bring the struggles against sexism and racism definitively together. Though as an abolitionist she had opposed slavery, she held, like her white contemporaries, unexamined racist attitudes. Her exuberance of moral passion was circumscribed by the blinders set on her vision by her whiteness. This fact in turn circumscribed the movement in which she worked so long and so hard.

Anthony always maintained that her persistence in the cause of women's rights, centering on the ballot, was fueled by her own self-respect, her refusal to be treated as a second-class human being. In celebrating her courage, her insistence on carrying the liberal values of the American Revolution one step further, we honor her best, I think, if we remind ourselves not only what her vision encompassed, but where it ended, and take up the challenge of pushing on.

I believe that my white sisters and I are challenged equally by Anthony's legacy and by the necessity to understand, for ourselves, the meanings of Black History Month. For without addressing the whiteness of white feminism, our movement will turn in on itself and collapse.

I start from the assumption that history is neither just a field of professionalization nor a "hobby" to be pursued through book clubs or antiquarian societies. As a woman, as a feminist, as a Jew, as a lesbian, I am pursued by questions of historical process, of historical responsibility, questions of historical consciousness and ignorance and what these have to do with power. And, as a poet, I would be unfaithful to my own trade if I did not recognize the debt that poetry owes to the historical impulse of oral tradition. Many of the enduring devices of the earliest written poetry were mnemonic in origin—repetitions of sound and phrase built into the structure of a narrative to assist memory, the first purpose of the poem being to keep alive

the memory of a people. Tribes and peoples throughout the
world have embodied this need for the past in poetry. So we
can speak of the debt that history owes to poets, not only in
terms of how memory is passed on orally and a heritage trans-
mitted, but in terms of how written poetry has kept history
alive. And I don't mean just the obvious—as how Chaucer's
Canterbury Tales evokes a vanished society—but the preserva-
tion of collective experience in poems like Thomas Hardy's
"Channel Firing," Claude McKay's "If We Must Die," Ran-
dall Jarrell's "The Lines" and "Losses," Kadia Molodowsky's
"White Night," Audre Lorde's "Afterimages," poems which
though individual and subjective speak for a whole community,
of world wars, of urban uprising, of the Holocaust, of lynching.
The novelist Doris Lessing has noted:

> We [Europeans] see history as events described in print. . . . To
> us a verbal tradition is not "history." A book written by a professor
> who has got his facts from the custodian of a verbal tradition is
> history, and is treated with respect. Only last week I heard a
> literary man say dismissingly of verbal records that "they contra-
> dict each other," just as if "historians"—that is, people who write
> books—don't contradict each other. . . . European nations have no
> verbal tradition in the sense that an African would understand it.
> Up and down Africa, history is kept carefully in the minds of black
> men and women chosen by their heredity, or because of their
> suitability, for this task. This is how history has always been kept
> by them, as record, story, legend, in traditions of healing, good
> government, the life of the tribe in nature.[1]

But history isn't just spoken words, verbal tradition either.
It has been transmitted through visual images—from the walls
of the Pyramids to the pictographs of Mesa Verde to the

---

1. Doris Lessing, "Lessing on Zimbabwe," *Doris Lessing Newsletter* 4, no. 1 (Sum-
mer 1980).

Bayeux tapestry to the battle paintings of Uccello to Diego Rivera's murals depicting the Spanish invasion of Mexico to the WPA murals painted in the thirties on the walls of courthouses and post offices—and through visual images it is coming to us still. Through the racist and sexist visual perspective of films like *Birth of a Nation* and *Gone with the Wind,* still hailed by white critics as great film classics; through the fascist lens of Leni Riefenstahl's *Triumph of the Will* (also classified as a great art film); through the compensatory history—still diminishing women—of television series like "Roots" or "Holocaust"; through the three-dimensional stage sets of Disneyland or Epcot, which propagandize on a gigantic scale for the dominant culture—the white, American, capitalist, straight, male version. History is not something we can take or leave: some representation of it is always being made to us under the guise of art or entertainment; some selected image of the past is always being delivered to our senses, even in the form of fashion and cosmetics, as in "Fifties Nostalgia." Sometimes these representations are quite honest in naming themselves: an advertisement in the *New Yorker* magazine for January 17, 1983, announces the Nostalgia Book Club:

> YES, I want to recapture the good old days. Please send my FREE copy of the current Nostalgia Bulletin and a membership application.

Nostalgia as history is nothing new; the Civil War, the 1890s have come in for a notable share of it. The Black playwright Lorraine Hansberry remarked that whole books have been written on the Civil War in which pages are devoted to the structure of battles and "which army was crossing the river at five minutes to two and how their swords were hanging," and in which slavery is never mentioned.[2] Nostalgia for the "Gay" Nineties comes complete with gaslight, looped velvet swags, mustache cups, marble-topped tables, and flamboyant robber barons, but it's a white man's nostalgia; it serves to deny and finally erase the discriminatory laws and practices against the Asian immigrant in romantic San Francisco, violence against Black women and men living under the neoslavery of the post-Reconstruction South, the brutal seizure of the Philippines by U.S. forces, immigrant white women working for women's wages (the lowest) in New York City sweatshops, sexual slaves in the northwestern lumber camps, the still continuing dispossession and genocide against American Indians, all common to that period. The nostalgia that allows these contradictions to slip through our fingers constitutes a peculiar philosophy of history—a philosophy of history that sees only certain kinds of human lives as valuable, as deserving of a history at all.

In the most recent issue of the feminist journal *Heresies*, there is a notable piece of art work: two sets of postage stamps, designed by the artist Janet Koenig. These are at first glance deceptively like real commemorative stamps; but one commemorates "Cotton Dust of Textile Mills: Women Fight Brown Lung," and the other, designed like a British stamp with the silhouette of Elizabeth II in the corner, depicts an immigrant woman of color walking past a wall bearing graffiti in chalk, "White Rule in U.K." Of these images, and her impulse to make them, Janet Koenig says:

> To question what is represented on postage stamps is to begin to imagine the history that has been left out.[3]

2. *Lorraine Hansberry Speaks Out: Art and the Black Revolution*, selected and ed. Robert Nemiroff (Caedmon recording TC 1352 [1972]).

3. Janet Koenig, "Commemorative Stamp Series," *Heresies: A Feminist Publication on Art and Politics* 4, no. 3 (1982): 8.

History as "advertisement for the state" (Koenig's phrase) has existed probably as long as the state has existed; it is a way of justifying the hands that already hold power, of proving that others are unfit for power, in part by making invisible or cruelly distorting their experience and culture. It is nothing new to say that history is the version of events told by the conqueror, the dominator. Even the dominators acknowledge this. What has more feelingly and pragmatically been said by people of color, by white women, by lesbians and gay men, by people with roots in the industrial or rural working class is that without our own history we are unable to imagine a future because we are deprived of the precious resource of knowing where we come from: the valor and the waverings, the visions and defeats of those who went before us. Joan Nestle, one of the founders and curators of the Lesbian Herstory Archives in New York City, has said:

> We need to know that we are not accidental, that our culture has grown and changed with the currents of time, that we like others have a social herstory, filled with individual lives, community struggles, and customs of language, dress and behavior that when looked at in their entirety form what we call herstory—the story of a people.[4]

To recover history, or herstory, means resisting two powerful pressures in present-day American culture—and, I suspect, in the culture being created globally by the multinational high-technology empires. These are very similar pressures, yet they are not the same. One is the imperative to assimilate; the other, the idea that one can be socially "twice-born." In its quest for a middle-class standard of life, every wave of immigrants who were not already Anglo-Saxon has been haunted by the pressure to assimilate. By constructing an ideal of Americanization

4. Joan Nestle, "Living with Herstory," *The Body Politic* (September 1983).

and equating this with virtue, progressiveness, decency, and worth, the assimilation imperative has also assured that those least able to assimilate—most often because of skin color or gender but also because of ethnicity or religion—could be cast as absolute Other, sentenced to live by different laws, treated as victims of inferior biology. The pressure to assimilate says different things to different people: change your name, your accent, your nose; straighten or dye your hair; stay in the closet; pretend the Pilgrims were your fathers; become baptized as a christian; wear dangerously high heels, and starve yourself to look young, thin, and feminine; don't gesture with your hands; value elite European culture above all others; laugh at jokes about your own people; don't make trouble; defer to white men; smile when they take your picture; be ashamed of who you are. To assimilate means to give up not only your history but your body, to try to adopt an alien appearance because your own is not good enough, to fear naming yourself lest name be twisted into label. Through this imperative, those who can "pass" are cheated of the chance to define themselves and to make mutually respectful and strengthening alliances with other self-defining people. It leaves them unanchored when storms arise, ignorant of their inheritance. Television programs on the Holocaust do not fill the need for an understanding of Jewish history and of the continuing history of anti-Semitism for both Jews and non-Jews. And if, as women, we accept a philosophy of history that asserts that women are by definition assimilated into the male universal, that we can understand *our* past through a male lens—if we are unaware that women even *have* a history—we live our lives similarly unanchored, drifting in response to a veering wind of myth and bias.

Joan Nestle suggests that "this gift of continuity carries its own burdens with it." She goes on to say that "having a herstory will certainly complicate issues because simplistic positions will seldom do justice to it." The desire to be twice-born is, I believe, in part a longing to escape the burdens, complications, and contradictions of continuity. The Christian fundamentalist model of the twice-born is of a soul once drenched in sin—in negativity—which through some charismatic encounter comes to see the truth, reject its former "path," confess its unworthiness, accept redemption, leave sin and shame behind, and take up a new "path" of innocence, cleansed by surrender to a higher being. But it is not only in Christian fundamentalism that we see this pattern traced. It's a very old American pattern, the pattern of the frontier, the escape from the old identity, the old debts, the old wife to the new name, the "new life." It's a pattern of contemporary cults, not only of Christianity—the changed garments, the shaven head perhaps, the new name, the obliteration of old connections, the surrender to an authority who promises to change your life. It has also been a pattern found in certain political communities—the denial, say, of one's class background if middle class, though often in its self-indulgence it insults the values of working-class people; the purity of the correct political line; the surrender to an authority who promises new life. And women's communities have not been exceptions to this pattern. In the desire to be twice-born there is a good deal of self-hatred. Too much of ourselves must be deleted when we erase our personal histories and abruptly dissociate ourselves from who we have been. We become less dimensional than we really are. The dialectic between change and continuity is a painful but deeply instructive one, in personal life as in the life of a people. To "see the light" too often has meant rejecting the treasures found in darkness.

As individuals, we sometimes find ourselves having to make

ruptures with the values or the people we grew up among, or
we may find ourselves forcibly shut out from our community
of origin, as so many lesbians and gay men have been. We may
know no other way to separate from parents, sisters, brothers,
lovers, husbands except awkwardly and violently, so great are
the pain and anger. But to deny that the connection ever
existed, to pretend that we have moved on a direct, single-
minded track—that is to subtract from ourselves the fullness
of what we are, and it also impoverishes others who have to go
the same route.

Collectively, an oppressed people may look back on their
history and recognize that there was not only oppression but
self-injury, that there was breaking of promises, injustice, de-
ceit; we can't have a history if we want only to hear the tales
of our best moments, our finest hours. White men, who more
than any other group have dominated this planet, have need
of a history that does not lie to them about the abuses of white
male power, the terrible skewing of behavior and psychic life
in a society dominated by a single-sex, racist, and profit per-
spective. White men need a history that does not simply "in-
clude" peoples of color and white women, but that shows the
process by which the arrogance of hierarchy and the celebra-
tion of violence have reached a point of destructiveness almost
out of control. In other words, white men need to start ques-
tioning the text handed down from father to son, the domina-
tor's version.

I hope that by now you realize what I am saying—that we
cannot help making history because we are made of it, and
history is made of people like us, carriers of the behavior and
assumptions of a given time and place. About this, the impact
of our individual existences, we have no choice. Whether I see
myself as a victim, as a harmless person, as stupid, as excep-
tional, as a monster (and the list could go on and on), I am born

both innocent and accountable. In his 1980 address to the Association for the Study of Afro-American Life and History, the Black historian Lerone Bennett spoke of history as

> the totalizing force that seizes you and throws you down here instead of there, with this color instead of that color, with this task instead of that task. . . . There is nothing you can do in history that will free you of the historical responsibility of being born at a certain time, in a certain place, with a certain skin color.[5]

I would add, of course, and into a certain sex. For women as a group and as individuals have historical responsibilities of our own which we can embrace or evade, but their consequences will affect us either way.

But you do have a choice to become *consciously* historical —that is, a person who tries for memory and connectedness against amnesia and nostalgia, who tries to describe her or his journeys as accurately as possible—or to become a technician of amnesia and nostalgia, one who dulls the imagination by starving it or feeding it junk food. Historical amnesia *is* starvation of the imagination; nostalgia is the imagination's sugar rush, leaving depression and emptiness in its wake. Breaking silences, telling our tales, is not enough. We can value that process—and the courage it may require—without believing that it is an end in itself. Historical responsibility has, after all, to do with action—where we place the weight of our existences on the line, cast our lot with others, move from an individual consciousness to a collective one. But we all need to begin with the individual consciousness: How did we come to be where we are and not elsewhere?

What, then, is the meaning of history if one is a woman? And what is feminist history? In asking these questions I have

5. *Ebony* (February 1981): 33–42.

found myself in a kind of dialogue with Lerone Bennett, from whom I quoted earlier. In his address, he asked two questions:

> What is the meaning of the Black odyssey in this land? Why are we here instead of there?

He went on to say that these were questions posed by the pioneer Black historians as well as by the great philosopher of Black history W. E. B. Du Bois, who asked: "What shall these things mean, O God the Reader?" And Bennett asserts that "the history of Afro-Americans is, among other things, the history of a quest for meaning." Taking notes on Bennett's address, I wrote: "True for women's history? If not, why not?" "What is the difference between women's history and feminist history?"

I would suggest that feminist history is history charged with meaning. Women's history, to be sure, always has a feminist potential. But, as Bennett observes, it is the historian who invests with meaning the history she or he writes or who may leave gaps in meaning, blur the focus. Feminist history charges us, as women committed to the liberation of women, to know the past in order to consider what we want to conserve and what we want not to repeat or continue. To see patterns, connections, which the false assimilation of liberal humanism obscures. To draw strength: Memory is nutriment, and seeds stored for centuries can still germinate. As differentiated from women's history, feminist history does not perpetuate the mainstream by simply invoking women to make the mainstream appear more inclusive. It is not simply contributory; it demands that we turn the questions upside down, that we ask women's questions where they have not been asked before. Feminist history is not history about women only; it looks afresh at what men have done and how they have behaved, not only toward women but toward each other and the natural world. But the central perspective and preoccupation *is female,* and this implies a vast shift in values and priorities.

We have seen over and over that white male historians in general have tended to dismiss any history they didn't themselves write, on the grounds that it is unserious, unscholarly, a fad, too "political," "merely" oral and thus unreliable. But women have been writing women's history—and feminist history—for several centuries; it is *not* a new invention, but it has been ignored, buried, erased over and over. Each new generation of feminists has been forced to document the most elementary exposition of the oppression of women yet again and also to repeat mistakes made by sisters of an earlier era. This is one of the eroding effects of amnesia: we cannot build on what has been done before because we do not even know it is there to build on.

In other ways as well, feminists have been caught in a hard place historically. Sheila Rowbotham, a British Marxist-feminist historian, comments of women that "we have no time or place to look back to. . . . We have not unravelled what we share and what is specific to us."[6] At the other end of the spectrum, Monique Wittig, in her lesbian-feminist utopian novel *Les Guérillères,* exhorts us, "Try to remember—or failing that, invent." Both statements suggest that we cannot lay claim with assurance to any motherland of the spirit, which might provide us with blueprints for a society in which women would be free, autonomous human beings. We have veered between believing that we have always and everywhere been the appendages or property of men, as man-made history implies, and heroinizing elite women such as Eleanor of Aqui-

6. Sheila Rowbotham, *Woman's Consciousness, Man's World* (London: Pelican, 1973), p. 36.

taine or Elizabeth I or "exceptional" strong women of an oppressed group—Sojourner Truth, Mother Jones, Harriet Tubman, Rosa Luxemburg—those few whose names have sifted down to us through the silences of history, while cultural feminism has tended to lean heavily upon traces and hints of Amazon or matriarchal cultures. I believe that we have a right to conjecture, a right to invent; but there is a difference between "inventing" a lost culture, as a kind of extended metaphor for yet unrealized values and visions, and making educated guesses, as every historian of an oppressed group must do. As feminists, we need to be looking above all for the greatness and sanity of ordinary women, and how these women have collectively waged resistance. In searching that territory we find something better than individual heroines: the astonishing continuity of women's imagination of survival, persisting through the great and little deaths of daily life.

I would say that the educated guess is essential to feminist history—and, in particular, to the history of women of color and/or lesbians because their lives have been the most undocumented in the literal sense. We have to be able to turn to what Audre Lorde, in her book *Zami,* calls "biomythography," exploring the worlds of West Indian immigrant women in New York City or of lesbians—Black and white—in a New England factory town, or in Mexico or the Greenwich Village of the 1950s. Or to the intuitions of Maxine Hong Kingston, who interpolates legend, family lore, legal research, and mythology to evoke the lives of her Chinese immigrant mother and father, grandmothers and grandfathers. Or to a novel, based on family papers, like Joy Kogawa's *Obasan.* It has seemed to me that Black women writers in particular have been creating a new kind of historical fiction, writing novels which are quite consciously intended as resources in Black women's history. The novelist Margaret Walker spent thirty years writing her novel

Jubilee, which traces a woman's odyssey through slavery, the Civil War, and Reconstruction, and which deserves the kind of reputation unfortunately held instead by *Gone with the Wind* and *Roots.* I'm thinking also of Alice Childress's *A Short Walk,* which takes its heroine from Charleston to Harlem, through the Garveyite era into the depression and World War II; of the novels of Buchi Emecheta, depicting women's lives in both pre- and postcolonial West Africa and as immigrants in Britain; of Michelle Cliff's novel *Abeng,* which moves back and forth between Jamaica of the 1950s and the slavery era, and the Harlem Renaissance. These novels are not romantic or nostalgic about the past. They share in common, for all their diversity, a consciously critical stance toward both white and male culture, and a respect for the courage and spiritual power of Black women which is far from sentimental. The women protagonists these authors create are individuals, for all they share in common. I think of these writers as historians who are making sure that the Black woman can no longer be severed from her context in history, who are making sure that she *has* a written history which will not be subsumed under the experience either of white women or of white or Black men.

Feminist history is history charged with meaning. It shows us images we have not seen before, throws new elements into relief. It is, indeed, as the department chairmen and the deans of liberal arts suspect, political. So, of course, is the history of white men, as told by themselves, political, having to do with the retention of power. And if we are serious about empowerment for women and about changing the very definitions of power, we need to know both the worst and the best. As far as possible, we need to know the full range and depth of how women have been controlled, the measure of anti-woman violence—we need the facts. And we need to know how and when and where women have resisted, and in what cultures and communities and periods women have had authority, control over vital resources, bargaining power, or leadership *as women* and not as honorary men. And we need very much to know how even under shared oppression, unequal privilege has kept us from sharing what powers we have had.

In a posthumously published essay on the first four centuries of French feminist debate known as the *querelle des femmes,* struck off by the writings of Christine de Pisan in the fourteenth and fifteenth centuries, Joan Kelly offers today's feminists both the sense of a longer written history than many of us had realized we possessed, and some parallels to—as well as divergences from—our own struggles. This early European feminism derived from the opportunities afforded by privilege; it was the response of some educated women to the "wearisome and obscene" woman loathing in the writings of the Humanists. As Kelly shows, it was also finally limited by the isolation of privilege. In their efforts to counter the Humanists' insistence on women's moral and intellectual inferiority, these women were well aware that "histories are constructed from a male position—and reinforce that position." But they believed that if they could only demonstrate rationally that women were capable of, and that some had achieved, intellectual stature and powers of leadership, misogyny would collapse under proof of its mistakes and social change would come about through enlightenment. In pursuit of such proofs, the early French feminists turned for models to famous learned women, to queens and aristocratic women and female warriors of the past. Kelly points out that, as a result, in an era when the power of women in general was declining ever more rapidly, these feminists "had little knowledge of the lives of most other women and did not look to them as a source of power. For all their fierce retorts to misogyny, for example, they never noticed its single most horrendous expression in early modern Europe, the hanging or

burning alive of some 100,000 or more women as witches."[7]
Had they done so, they might have felt impelled to move from
theory to activism and to wider definitions of women and
power.

As we claim our history as women, feminism demands that
we give attention not only to patriarchal misogyny, but also to
the chauvinisms of ethnicity and class and heterosexuality
which prevent us from "seeing" whole groups of women. As
long as we separate the history of white and middle-class
women from the history of colored and poor women we are not
only missing powerful lines of insight, we are perpetuating our
own fragmentation. It is a feminist view of history that de-
mands new texts—what Joan Kelly called a new periodization
and what I would call a new cultural orientation—that will save
women's history from trickling into the history books as mere
lists of names appended to history-as-usual. A new cultural
orientation may help us, as women, not to write books in which
other women's lives are misconstrued or ignored.

You can't escape history because it is everywhere. The blue
jeans we wear are part of it, long stitched by women in the
nonunionized factories of the American South, now also in the
nonunionized shops of the Philippines, South Korea, In-
donesia, Malaysia, Taiwan, Thailand. An international female
proletariat of textile workers continues today, as it has since the
industrial revolution. As we reclaim metaphors of women weav-
ers and spinners, and the word *spinster* itself; as we sing the
"Bread and Roses" anthem of the nineteenth-century Law-
rence, Massachusetts, mill girls; as we search with awe and
pride into the flare and authority of women's imaginations
translated into quilts, and study the histories secreted in colors,

7. Joan Kelly, *Women, History and Theory* (Chicago: Chicago University Press,
1984), pp. 93–94.

stitches, materials; as we write our elegies for the women burned to death in the Triangle Shirtwaist Fire, let us not fail to be aware of the history still being played out by "the nineteen year old Filipino woman sewing the difficult side seam along the denim cloth of a Levi's blue jean pant leg in a new industrial zone outside Manila." According to political scientist Cynthia Enloe, "Today women textile workers in the industrialized countries are being encouraged by male businessmen, labor leaders and government officials to see Third World women textile workers as their enemies, and threats to their jobs, as low-paid and exploitative as those jobs may be."[8] This is happening in an era which has been called the decade of the "feminization of poverty" in which the U.S. Commission on Civil Rights has recently released a report showing that job discrimination against white women and Black and Hispanic women and men persists at an "alarming" rate, at *every* age level, at *every* educational level, at *every* skills level. If it is the present that calls us to activism, it is history that must nourish our choices and commitment.

A few weeks ago, at a workshop in Florida, at a college not unlike the Claremont Colleges in its almost romantic physical beauty, a young white man asked me, "Don't you think women have enough equality *now that* the ERA has passed?" I have since thought a great deal about the sense of history that that question implies. What it suggests to me is not just amnesia, but the ignorance that a privileged existence can permit. If men can afford to be ignorant of the political struggles of women, if they find them either so insignificant or so threatening that they choose to remain uninformed, this is itself another mark of the absolute necessity of women's efforts to place

8. Cynthia Enloe, "Women Textile Workers in the Militarization of Southeast Asia," paper for the Conference on Perspectives on Power: Women in Asia, Africa and Latin America, Duke University, March 1981.

themselves in history, to "know where we are." Each woman
and man in this room is constantly making a choice, to know
or not to know, to fight if necessary for the past that has been
withheld from us or to remain ignorant, hoping perhaps that
"if I don't know, I won't have to move." And these individual
choices do add up, become what will later be defined as the
history of this decade, those years, that group of people.

We live—and we are the first generation of feminists, of
activists, of history makers and history writers to live—in a
society which has brought the entire planet to the brink of
having no future. We are experiencing a kind of global anger
and grief which we do not always name for what it is or know
how to name. But I think we must live taking thought for the
future, both in the sense of waging opposition to military-
industrial madness and the mental systems that produce it, and
in the sense of hoping audaciously, refusing to be made into
victims, willing the future into being. In the words of Lerone
Bennett, "We are more in chaos without a history, than we are
without a future."

I want to end with some concrete proposals: What do we do
in our lives now? As students, you can ask yourselves and your
teachers: What is missing, *who* is missing, in the versions of
history, the canons of literature, we are being taught? You can
refuse to be put off from Women's Studies courses by the fear
of being identified as feminists, by the fear that you may learn
things which will make you angry, by the fear that you will not
be seen as a serious student. When you are enrolled in courses
in the study of women, you can ask yourselves: *Which* women
are being talked about? White women only? Women attached
to middle- and upper-class men? Heterosexual women only?
Black and white women, without reference to women of Asian,
American Indian, Latina origin? Where are the Jewish
women? The Arab women? Black and white in this country

have a long and specific history together, but Black and white
are not the only colors used to discriminate against and select
among people. You can question generalizations which are
made from a white perspective as if they applied to all women.
You can, at the same time, be searching for the patterns of
history shared by women everywhere.

As teachers, we have to become students again, continually.
We have to do what workers on any intellectual frontier have
always had to do: push beyond the limits of our training, look
to new kinds of sources. In the contemporary feminist move-
ment, we have more than thirteen years behind us of theory,
research, documentation, testimony, as well as poetry, fiction,
philosophy, drama, graphic arts, music, and anthologies of all
of these. Much, though not all, of this work has been published
in feminist and lesbian-feminist periodicals, and by feminist
and lesbian-feminist publishing houses such as Daughters, Inc.,
Shameless Hussy Press, Naiad Press, The Feminist Press,
Persephone Press, Kitchen Table/Women of Color Press,
Long Haul Press, Spinsters Ink, and Firebrand Books. Much
of it is hard to find unless you make regular visits to a women's
bookstore, subscribe to feminist periodicals, get your name on
mailing lists. Beside the feminist scholarly work continually
appearing, there are the life and debate and ongoing struggles
of a political movement about which we can read virtually
nothing in the mainstream press unless a scandal is unearthed
or a major defeat occurs. One answer to this would be to form
study groups, journal clubs, with each member responsible for
reporting on the contents of several feminist publications a
month. Women's Studies cannot survive without a strong
relatedness to the grass-roots movement out of which it came,
and to the pragmatic experience of women out of which femi-
nist theory was born and continues to grow. Our theory, schol-
arship, and teaching must continue to refer back to flesh,

blood, violence, sexuality, anger, the bread put on the table by the single mother and how it gets there, the body of the woman aging, the pregnant body, the body running, the body limping, the hands of the lesbian touching another lesbian's face, the hands of the typist, of the midwife, of the sewing-machine operator, the eyes of the woman astronomer, of the woman going blind on the transistor assembly line, of the mother catching the briefest expression on the child's face: the particularity and commonality of this vast turbulence of female becoming, which is continually being erased or generalized.

This weekend a Women's Studies conference will be held here in Claremont, and beginning a week from Sunday a week-long conference on violence against women. Both events confirm that it is a basic act of self-respect to refuse to acquiesce in our own derogation and dehumanization; to decide that we will not surrender our bodies or our minds without a struggle, that we will not be bought, or battered, or teased, or terrorized, or numbed, or brain-starved into any state which mutilates our integrity. And to say yes, over and over, to our integrity, we need to know where we have been: we need our history.

"Going There" and Being Here (1983)

For some time before I went to Nicaragua, I had been thinking about the fact that U.S. feminism is after all rooted in North America, within a technologically powerful and malevolent political system, and about the problems and dangers of seeing our particular issues as some kind of model or vanguard for women everywhere. (This is a common North American, Euro-American, form of chauvinism.) It has seemed important to me that as a movement we gain some conscious perspective on this, allowing us to see ourselves as a self-respecting and self-critical part of one great movement for freedom among others, all interdependent. I went to Nicaragua partly to test these thoughts against a concrete reality. While there, I went through moments of feeling contradictions—both within feminism and within the Sandinista revolution—like a physical pain: not just the sensation of being torn apart, but also of long-severed pieces wrenching back together. And there were moments—watching day break over green hills from a bus en

Originally published in off our backs. *Reprinted in* Nicaraguan Women: Unlearning the Alphabet of Submission *(New York: Women's International Resource Exchange [WIRE], 1985)*.

route to the Honduran border—of astonishing, simple happiness.

At the Conference on Central America in Nicaragua last July, I felt the absurdity of traveling to a four-year-old, evolving, U.S.-beleaguered society, carrying in hand an agenda from U.S. feminism to which we expect that society to answer or be written off. Listening to and learning from the women and men dedicated to creating a new Nicaraguan society felt more urgent, more necessary to my own feminist politics than pressing questions like abortion, which is still illegal there. (Contraceptives are free on demand; no anti-gay laws exist, and none is contemplated.)[1] The issue of women's rights to our bodies is, of course, not just a U.S. priority; it's a global one. But how different women engage with these issues, under many different forms of patriarchy, is being determined by the women of each and every movement for social change.

Contrary to impressions conveyed in the U.S. media, the Sandinista revolution is not a clone of the Soviet or Chinese or Cuban revolution, though ties with both Cuba and Grenada are naturally close.[2] A great variety of ideas are in ferment; the Sandinistas speak of trying to create their own kind of revolution, learning both from older revolutions and from their own mistakes. If the economic and military onslaughts of the United States against this young and fragile process lead to an emphasis on defensive measures against counterrevolution, this is not where the Sandinistas would like to be putting their energy. The leadership of women in the armed rebellion

---

1. [A.R., 1986: As this book goes to press, the citizens of Nicaragua are discussing and creating the new constitution. Within this process, a debate on sexuality—specifically, abortion rights and homosexuality—is going on, with AMNLAE (the Luisa Amanda Espinosa Association of Nicaraguan Women) actively raising these questions ("A Frank Discussion: Sex and the Sandinistas," *The Guardian* [May 21, 1986], p. 17).]

2. This article was written before the U.S. invasion of Grenada in November 1983.

against Somoza's U.S.-supported fascism was generated by a history of strong Nicaraguan women, often raising children alone, working to support their families, learning to depend on their own courage and staying power. I trust such women to go on setting their own priorities. In a society born in poverty, menaced from without, the priority at this moment is life itself and the protection of a revolution which spells hope after decades of terror and deprivation.

Another thing I realized concretely while there: If you are trying to transform a brutalized society into one where people can live in dignity and hope, you begin with the empowering of the most powerless. You build from the ground up. You begin by stopping the torture and killing of the unprotected, by feeding the hungry so that they have the energy to think about what they want beyond food. The Sandinistas are committed to providing all citizens with basic nutrition, have cut the illiteracy rate in half, have wiped out polio and made a huge dent in the infant mortality rate. *These elementary things change women's lives.* Food, health, literacy, like free contraception and abortion, are basic feminist issues.

As a feminist, I can feel skeptical of phrases like "the integration of women into the Revolution"—a much-used phrase. As a U.S. citizen, I have learned to be skeptical of false integrations. But the process of "integrating women into the Revolution" is substantially different from the attempt to get some women "integrated" into the upper-level executive or professional world in a capitalist patriarchy. Within the process of revolution, the middle-class housewife and the poor market woman have a chance to meet, work together, and explore what they have in common as women, what needs they share as women that are not being met. "Integration" of a few women into capitalist patriarchy only deepens the trenches between women.

In the late sixties and early seventies many U.S. feminists, myself included, voiced frustration and disillusionment with the Marxist Left, which seemed incapable of recognizing and addressing women's oppression as women. We insisted that our chains were not only economic but mental, embedded in that domestic or "private" sphere where men of all classes dominate women. I believe we were right: no ideology which reduces women simply to members of the working class or the bourgeoisie, which does not recognize how central feminism must be to revolutionary process, can be taken seriously any longer. But also, in the past decade, "radical feminists," "socialist feminists," "lesbian feminists" have been pulling at each other, stretching each other's minds, eavesdropping on each other, learning from each other more than we often admit. Women of color have often been the catalyst for these connections, and the chief exponents of the evolving consciousness.

I came home from Nicaragua convinced that white feminists need to keep defining and describing our relationship both to capitalism and to socialism, and to talk seriously about our place in the interconnecting movements for bread, self-determination, dignity, and justice. And I came home feeling that feminists in the United States, *because we are here,* have a special reason to help try to get the foot of the United States off Central America. The women of Central America will then have room to move and name their own priorities as women, and this possibility affects us all.[3]

3. [A.R., 1986: For a more recent and searching account of six months in Nicaragua by a Jewish lesbian feminist, see Rebecca Gordon, *Letters from Nicaragua* (San Francisco: Spinsters/Aunt Lute Books, 1986).]

North American Tunnel Vision (1983)

Never has a meeting like this felt more necessary, more inevitable. During the past several weeks the movie has been speeding up, the bulletins coming in faster and faster, seemingly disconnected: Korean jet crashes, black box is searched for, suddenly we hear no more; CIA openly admits financing, supplying, and supervising commando raids on Nicaragua even as the Sandinista government is trying to initiate peaceful negotiations; over 200 U.S. Marines blown up in Lebanon, no one really knows why; a coup wipes out the leadership of Grenada, a government with close bonds both to Cuba and to the Sandinistas, U.S. Marines invade the island, and even now the cover-up stories are being marketed; the president of the United States contemptuously signs a bill declaring the birthday of Martin Luther King a national holiday and flies off to a segregated golf course in Georgia. In Europe, millions of people covering a vast political spectrum demonstrate against U.S. and Soviet missile deployment. Our government keeps

Talk given in New York City at "Women in Struggle," an evening sponsored by I-KON *magazine, October 28, 1983. First published in* Gay Community News *(Boston), November 26, 1983.*

telling us that its thumbprint of violence all over the world is for our protection, our national interests and security. Yet in this free country, in this city of art and culture and "free" enterprise, men and women are picking their food from the garbage cans on Broadway. In this advanced technological society, 40 percent of all adults can barely read and 20 percent are functionally illiterate.[1] In this city, as across the country, Black and Hispanic women and men, and white women are living in the very basement of the economy, a whole generation of youth is being wasted by neglect and violence, while a generation of elders—72 percent of them women—is dying in poverty, forgotten. In this city, where so many cultures struggle to persist, to hang on to their vitality, where women are, as everywhere, the linchpin of the economy, where the strength of women is the deep undercurrent of all life, we have come to try to connect what we know and what we do.

I'm supposed to talk about my trip to Nicaragua. I have taken that assignment in a very loose sense. First, although the week I spent there last July was a process of continuous adult education for me, this process was itself connected with a much longer political education. It would be easier if I could describe a conversion: how an on-the-spot visit to a Central American revolutionary society affected my politics as a feminist. In fact, "my trip to Nicaragua" feels spread over months and years.

I went quite unexpectedly, though in some ways I had been heading there a long time. I had been to no Latin American country except Mexico. But I had been meeting women from Argentina, Puerto Rico, Chile who were feminists and political dissenters, and through whom my hemispheric education

1. President Derek Bok of Harvard University cited these figures in his annual report to the alumni. See *Harvard Magazine* (Summer 1983).

began. I had for six months been reading Margaret Randall's *Breaking the Silences,* an anthology of twentieth-century Cuban women poets, which had tremendous impact on me. And I had for a long time been struggling, along with other white feminists, with the meanings of white identity in a racist society and how an unexamined white perspective leads to dangerous ignorance, heart-numbing indifference, and complacency. As a Jew, I had also been trying, with other Jewish feminists, to explore the meanings of Jewish identity from a feminist perspective. A natural extension of all this seemed to me the need to examine not only racial and ethnic identity, but *location* in the United States of North America. As a feminist in the United States it seemed necessary to examine how we participate in mainstream North American cultural chauvinism, the sometimes unconscious belief that white North Americans possess a superior right to judge, select, and ransack other cultures, that we are more "advanced" than other peoples of this hemisphere. (And this cultural chauvinism is constantly feeding itself on racism.) Even as we have analyzed and rejected patriarchal chauvinism, even as we try to disengage ourselves from its destructive principles and to express other values, we carry in us—I had been finding in myself—not only a white but a specifically North American tunnel vision. It was not enough to say "As a woman I have no country; as a woman my country is the whole world." Magnificent as that vision may be, we can't explode into its breadth without a conscious grasp on the particular and concrete meaning of our location here and now, in the United States of America.

So, when out of the blue came an invitation to a conference in Managua on Central America, I went. I went down with questions—about the Miskito Indians, about the Jewish community, about legislation on homosexuality, above all about women. I went feeling torn between the urgency of the questions of these various communities and the urgency of understanding what the Sandinistas believed they were doing. I found myself having to think about "women's issues" not just as reproductive issues or the problems of rape, woman battering, child abuse, but as literacy, infant mortality, the fundamental issue of having something to eat. I had written about the bedrock significance of hunger as a feminist issue. But to hear this issue addressed repeatedly by members of a government was something new. On a global scale I still believe that "the decision to feed the world" cannot be extricated from the liberation of women. But in Nicaragua, this tiny, impoverished, economically besieged country, trying through its own fragile means to feed itself, it is easy to see that women's ability to liberate themselves from social roles and domestic bondage cannot precede their ability to feed themselves and their children, and their access to basic resources.

Meeting daily with the women and men who are responsible for day-to-day policy decisions in that revolution the United States is so determined to overturn, I found myself constantly having to remind myself that these *were* members of the government. We are not used to seeing and hearing people at the highest levels of government who sound as if they believe what they are saying, who speak with love and commitment to the needs of the poorest people, who speak of their country in a language of concrete, unaggrandized simplicity—of its sufferings, its hopes, its beauty, its poverty, its smallness, its need to work out its own way in the world. The acknowledgment that in the process of revolution, so newly begun, mistakes have been made, injuries inflicted, that the defeat of dictatorship does not give instant birth to new human beings, that people trying to reconstruct a battered society are not free of old chauvinisms—and that there must be continuing openness to criticism. But what most entered my heart and soul, in that brief time of being in the physical presence of a revolutionary process, was the quality I think we are all here tonight trying to affirm—hope. The sense that *it can change. We ourselves can change it.* [2]

North Americans are so used to living in a naïve cynicism. We shrug at the manipulations which are the daily life of this society; we do not expect sincerity in public life. Yet the United States is not a country most of whose citizens are used to thinking of their government as inimical to them, even when we can see all around us the lying, the contempt, the neglect of needs. We have spent forty years as a people—the whole of many people's lives—immersed in Cold War rhetoric, images of a brutish and virulent communism whose hostility is our most urgent national burden. Most of us have grown up with messages telling us to focus on the enemy without, not on the violence and indifference our government visits on its own citizens, the manic self-assertion of privilege it defines as "national interest." The United States has been for decades deep-frozen in the Cold War, unable to move freely and responsively in the currents of history. And how could the feminist movement in this United States not share this nightmare, any more than it could not share in the nightmare of racism?

Patriarchy is no more an abstraction than imperialism is, once you have tasted it in your mouth, felt it across your flesh. The primary issues, the priorities, of feminists in the United States are not the offspring of bourgeois decadence. They have evolved through the hard and often dangerous work of thousands of courageous and radical women. Feminists have defined and organized around areas hitherto not even perceived as political: marital rape, abortion and sterilization

2. See Nancy Morejón's poem "Elogia de la Dialéctica," in *Breaking the Silences: Twentieth Century Poetry by Cuban Women,* ed. Margaret Randall (1982, Pulp Press, 3868 MPO, Vancouver, Canada V6B 3Z3).

abuse, sexual abuse in the family, sexual harassment in the workplace, education, religion, the oppression of lesbians, female health care, motherhood. We are far from having solved these problems, but we have identified and documented them and learned a great deal in organizing around them. In the process, women of diverse class, sexual, ethnic identities have had to come together. More than a decade of feminist organizing has brought us to this historical moment.

I want to suggest that United States feminism has a peculiar potential to break out of the nightmare and place itself more intelligently with other liberation movements (often led by women from whom we have much to learn) because the spiritual and moral vision of the United States women's movement is increasingly being shaped by women of color. The concepts of identity politics, of simultaneity of oppressions, of concrete experience as the touchstone for ideology, the refusal to accept "a room of one's own" in exchange for not threatening the system—these have been explored, expanded on, given voice most articulately by women of color, and to say this is not to set up competitions or divisions, but to acknowledge a precious resource, along with an indebtedness, that we can all share.

Because we have a multiracial movement deeply scarred by the blade of racism and ethnic chauvinism, because as North Americans of whatever background we inherit this diversity and the resulting intersections of oppression, the leadership— I could call it *teachership*—of women of color both impels and enables us to enter into nonchauvinistic, nonmissionary alliances with those around the world who refuse to abandon hope, who refuse to be dehumanized, who are trying to become more human. We have to assume that people do change, that feminism is changing, that socialism is changing, that the liberation movements will teach and learn from each other.

I repeat that United States feminists need to be very clear as to the particular patriarchy in which they are situated. But they also belong to a country in which the original Americans, the first victims of white expansionism, undermining of cultures, and destabilizing of whole societies have somehow retained identity and memory, and still assert the original values which connected their people to this land; a country in which African slaves and freedpeople and their descendants synthesized an old/new culture which has ennobled the alien society in whose despite it grew; in which generations of poor, Jewish, foreign-born, colored, and working people have survived—in large part through the anger and tenacious love of the women. There is every reason for United States women—especially feminists—to place themselves unmistakably alongside the freedom movements fermenting around the world in this late twentieth century, with all that that involves of new learning, confusion, conflict, the splitting open of meaning yet again in our politics and in our lives.

Blood, Bread, and Poetry: The Location of the Poet (1984)

The Miami airport, summer 1983: a North American woman says to me, "You'll love Nicaragua: everyone there is a poet." I've thought many times of that remark, both while there and since returning home. Coming from a culture (North American, white- and male-dominated) which encourages poets to think of ourselves as alienated from the sensibility of the general population, which casually and devastatingly marginalizes us (so far, no slave labor or torture for a political poem—just dead air, the white noise of the media jamming the poet's words)—coming from this North American dominant culture which so confuses us, telling us poetry is neither economically profitable nor politically effective and that political dissidence is destructive to art, coming from this culture that tells me I am destined to be a luxury, a decorative garnish on the buffet table of the university curriculum, the ceremonial occasion, the national celebration—what am I to make, I thought, of that remark? *You'll love Nicaragua: everyone there is a poet.* (Do I

Talk given for the Institute for the Humanities, University of Massachusetts, Amherst, series "Writers and Social Responsibility," 1983. Originally published in the Massachusetts Review.

love poets in general? I immediately asked myself, thinking of poets I neither love nor would wish to see in charge of my country.) Is being a poet a guarantee that I will love a Marxist-Leninist revolution? Can't I travel simply as an American radical, a lesbian feminist, a citizen who opposes her government's wars against its own people and its intervention in other people's lands? And what effectiveness has the testimony of a poet returning from a revolution where "everyone is a poet" to a country where the possible credibility of poetry is not even seriously discussed?

Clearly, this well-meant remark triggered strong and complex feelings in me. And it provided, in a sense, the text on which I began to build my talk here tonight.

I was born at the brink of the Great Depression; I reached sixteen the year of Nagasaki and Hiroshima. The daughter of a Jewish father and a Protestant mother, I learned about the Holocaust first from newsreels of the liberation of the death camps. I was a young white woman who had never known hunger or homelessness, growing up in the suburbs of a deeply segregated city in which neighborhoods were also dictated along religious lines: Christian and Jewish. I lived sixteen years of my life secure in the belief that though cities could be bombed and civilian populations killed, the earth stood in its old indestructible way. The process through which nuclear annihilation was to become a part of all human calculation had already begun, but we did not live with that knowledge during the first sixteen years of my life. And a recurrent theme in much poetry I read was the indestructibility of poetry, the poem as a vehicle for personal immortality.

I had grown up hearing and reading poems from a very young age, first as sounds, repeated, musical, rhythmically satisfying in themselves, and the power of concrete, sensuously compelling images:

All night long they hunted
   And nothing did they find
But a ship a-sailing,
   A-sailing with the wind.
One said it was a ship,
   The other he said, Nay,
The third said it was a house
   With the chimney blown away;
And all the night they hunted
   And nothing did they find
But the moon a-gliding
   A-gliding with the wind. . . .

Tyger! Tyger! burning bright
   In the forest of the night,
What immortal hand or eye
   Dare frame thy fearful symmetry?

But poetry soon became more than music and images; it was
also revelation, information, a kind of teaching. I believed I
could learn from it—an unusual idea for a United States citi-
zen, even a child. I thought it could offer clues, intimations,
keys to questions that already stalked me, questions I could not
even frame yet: *What is possible in this life? What does "love"
mean, this thing that is so important? What is this other thing
called "freedom" or "liberty"—is it like love, a feeling? What
have human beings lived and suffered in the past? How am I
going to live my life?* The fact that poets contradicted them-
selves and each other didn't baffle or alarm me. I was avid for
everything I could get; my child's mind did not shut down for
the sake of consistency.

I was angry with my friend,
I told my wrath, my wrath did end.
I was angry with my foe,
I told it not, my wrath did grow.

As an angry child, often urged to "curb my temper," I used to ponder those words of William Blake, but they slid first into my memory through their repetitions of sound, their ominous rhythms.

Another poem that I loved first as music, later pondered for what it could tell me about women and men and marriage, was Edwin Arlington Robinson's "Eros Turannos":

> She fears him, and will always ask
> What fated her to choose him;
> She meets in his engaging mask
> All reasons to refuse him;
> But what she meets and what she fears
> Are less than are the downward years,
> Drawn slowly to the foamless weirs
> Of age, were she to lose him. . . .

And, of course, I thought that the poets in the anthologies were the only real poets, that their being in the anthologies was proof of this, though some were classified as "great" and others as "minor." I owed much to those anthologies: *Silver Pennies;* the constant outflow of volumes edited by Louis Untermeyer; *The Cambridge Book of Poetry for Children;* Palgrave's *Golden Treasury;* the *Oxford Book of English Verse.* But I had no idea that they reflected the taste of a particular time or of particular kinds of people. I still believed that poets were inspired by some transcendent authority and spoke from some extraordinary height. I thought that the capacity to hook syllables together in a way that heated the blood was the sign of a universal vision.

Because of the attitudes surrounding me, the aesthetic ideology with which I grew up, I came into my twenties believing in poetry, in all art, as the expression of a higher world view, what the critic Edward Said has termed "a quasi-religious wonder, instead of a human sign to be understood in secular and social terms."[1] The poet achieved "universality" and authority through tapping his, or occasionally her, own dreams, longings, fears, desires, and, out of this, "speaking as a man to men," as Wordsworth had phrased it. But my personal world view at sixteen, as at twenty-six, was itself being created by political conditions. I was not a man; I was white in a white-supremacist society; I was being educated from the perspective of a particular class; my father was an "assimilated" Jew in an anti-Semitic world, my mother a white southern Protestant; there were particular historical currents on which my consciousness would come together, piece by piece. My personal world view was shaped in part by the poetry I had read, a poetry written almost entirely by white Anglo-Saxon men, a few women, Celts and Frenchmen notwithstanding. Thus, no poetry in the Spanish language or from Africa or China or the Middle East. My personal world view, which like so many young people I carried as a conviction of my own uniqueness, was not original with me, but was, rather, my untutored and half-conscious rendering of the facts of blood and bread, the social and political forces of my time and place.

I was in college during the late 1940s and early 1950s. The thirties, a decade of economic desperation, social unrest, war, and also of affirmed political art, was receding behind the fogs of the Cold War, the selling of the nuclear family with the mother at home as its core, heightened activity by the FBI and CIA, a retreat by many artists from so-called "protest" art, witch-hunting among artists and intellectuals as well as in the State Department, anti-Semitism, scapegoating of homosexual men and lesbians, and with a symbolic victory for the Cold War crusade in the 1953 electrocution of Ethel and Julius Rosenberg.

1. Edward Said, "Literature As Values," *New York Times Book Review* (September 4, 1983), p. 9.

Francis Otto Matthiessen, a socialist and a homosexual, was teaching literature at Harvard when I came there. One semester he lectured on five poets: Blake, Keats, Byron, Yeats, and Stevens. That class perhaps affected my life as a poet more than anything else that happened to me in college. Matthiessen had a passion for language, and he read aloud, made us memorize poems and recite them to him as part of the course. He also actually alluded to events in the outside world, the hope that eastern Europe could survive as an independent socialist force between the United States and the Soviet Union; he spoke of the current European youth movements as if they should matter to us. Poetry, in his classroom, never remained in the realm of pure textual criticism. Remember that this was in 1947 or 1948, that it was a rare teacher of literature at Harvard who referred to a world beyond the text, even though the classrooms were full of World War II veterans studying on the G.I. Bill of Rights—men who might otherwise never have gone to college, let alone Harvard, at all. Matthiessen committed suicide in the spring of my sophomore year.

Because of Yeats, who by then had become my idea of the Great Poet, the one who more than others could hook syllables together in a way that heated my blood, I took a course in Irish history. It was taught by a Boston Irish professor of Celtic, one of Harvard's tokens, whose father, it was said, had been a Boston policeman. He read poetry aloud in Gaelic and in English, sang us political ballads, gave us what amounted to a mini-education on British racism and imperialism, though the words were never mentioned. He also slashed at Irish self-romanticizing. People laughed about the Irish history course, said it must be full of football players. In and out of the Harvard Yard, the racism of Yankee Brahmin toward Boston Irish was never questioned, laced as it was with equally unquestioned class arrogance. Today, Irish Boston both acts out and takes the weight of New England racism against Black and Hispanic people. It was, strangely enough, through poetry that I first began to try to make sense of these things.

"Strangely enough," I say, because the reading of poetry in an elite academic institution is supposed to lead you—in the 1980s as back there in the early 1950s—not toward a criticism of society, but toward a professional career in which the anatomy of poems is studied dispassionately. Prestige, job security, money, and inclusion in an exclusive fraternity are where the academic study of literature is supposed to lead. Maybe I was lucky because I had started reading poetry so young, and not in school, and because I had been writing poems almost as long as I had been reading them. I should add that I was easily entranced by pure sound and still am, no matter what it is saying; and any poet who mixes the poetry of the actual world with the poetry of sound interests and excites me more than I am able to say. In my student years, it was Yeats who seemed to do this better than anyone else. There were lines of Yeats that were to ring in my head for years:

> Many times man lives and dies
> Between his two eternities,
> That of race and that of soul,
> And ancient Ireland knew it all. . . .
>
> Did she in touching that lone wing
> Recall the years before her mind
> Became a bitter, an abstract thing
> Her thought some popular enmity:
> Blind and leader of the blind
> Drinking the foul ditch where they lie?

I could hazard the guess that all the most impassioned, seductive arguments against the artist's involvement in politics can be found in Yeats. It was this dialogue between art and politics that excited me in his work, along with the sound of his language—never his elaborate mythological systems. I know I learned two things from his poetry, and those two things were at war with each other. One was that poetry can be "about," can root itself in, politics. Even if it is a defense of privilege, even if it deplores political rebellion and revolution, it can, may have to, account for itself politically, consciously situate itself amid political conditions, without sacrificing intensity of language. The other, that politics leads to "bitterness" and "abstractness" of mind, makes women shrill and hysterical, and is finally a waste of beauty and talent: "Too long a sacrifice / can make a stone of the heart." There was absolutely nothing in the literary canon I knew to counter the second idea. Elizabeth Barrett Browning's anti-slavery and feminist poetry, H.D.'s anti-war and woman-identified poetry, like the radical—yes, revolutionary—work of Langston Hughes and Muriel Rukeyser, were still buried by the academic literary canon. But the first idea was extremely important to me: a poet —one who was apparently certified—could actually write about political themes, could weave the names of political activists into a poem:

> MacDonagh and MacBride
> And Connally and Pearce
> Now and in time to come
> Wherever green is worn
> Are changed, changed utterly:
> A terrible beauty is born.

As we all do when young and searching for what we can't even name yet, I took what I could use where I could find it. When the ideas or forms we need are banished, we seek their residues wherever we can trace them. But there was one major problem with this. I had been born a woman, and I was trying to think and act as if poetry—and the possibility of making poems—were a universal—a gender-neutral—realm. In the universe of the masculine paradigm, I naturally absorbed ideas about women, sexuality, power from the subjectivity of male poets—Yeats not least among them. The dissonance between these images and the daily events of my own life demanded a constant footwork of imagination, a kind of perpetual translation, and an unconscious fragmentation of identity: woman from poet. Every group that lives under the naming and image-making power of a dominant culture is at risk from this mental fragmentation and needs an art which can resist it.

But at the middle of the fifties I had no very clear idea of my positioning in the world or even that such an idea was an important resource for a writer to have. I knew that marriage and motherhood, experiences which were supposed to be truly womanly, often left me feeling unfit, disempowered, adrift. But I had never had to think about bread itself as a primary issue; and what I knew of blood was that mine was white and that white was better off. Much as my parents had worried about questions of social belonging and acceptability, I had never had to swallow rage or humiliation to earn a paycheck. The literature I had read only rarely suggested that for many people it is a common, everyday fact of life to be hungry. I thought I was well educated. In that Cold War atmosphere, which has never really ended, we heard a lot about the "indoctrinating" of people in the Soviet Union, the egregious rewriting of history to conform to Communist dogma. But, like most Americans, I had been taught a particular version of our history, the version of the propertied white male; and in my early twenties I did not even realize this. As a younger and then an older woman, growing up in the white mainstream American culture, I was destined to piece together, for the rest of my life, laboriously and with much in my training against me, the history that really concerned me, on which I was to rely as a poet, the only history upon which, both as a woman and a poet, I could find any grounding at all: the history of the dispossessed.

It was in the pain and confusion of that inward wrenching of the self, which I experienced directly as a young woman in the fifties, that I started to feel my way backward to an earlier splitting, the covert and overt taboos against Black people, which had haunted my earliest childhood. And I began searching for some clue or key to life, not only in poetry but in political writers. The writers I found were Mary Wollstonecraft, Simone de Beauvoir, and James Baldwin. Each of them helped me to realize that what had seemed simply "the way things are" could actually be a social construct, advantageous to some people and detrimental to others, and that these constructs could be criticized and changed. The myths and obsessions of gender, the myths and obsessions of race, the violent exercise of power in these relationships could be identified, their territories could be mapped. They were not simply part of my private turmoil, a secret misery, an individual failure. I did not yet know what I, a white woman, might have to say about the racial obsessions of white consciousness. But I did begin to resist the apparent splitting of poet from woman, thinker from woman, and to write what I feared was political poetry. And in this I had very little encouragement from the literary people I knew, but I did find courage and vindication in words like Baldwin's: "Any real change implies the breakup of the world as one has always known it, the loss of all that gave one an identity, the end of safety." I don't know why I found these words encouraging—perhaps because they made me feel less alone.

Mary Wollstonecraft had seen eighteenth-century middle-class Englishwomen brain-starved and emotionally malnourished through denial of education; her plea was to treat women's minds as respectfully as men's—to admit women as equals into male culture. Simone de Beauvoir showed how the male perception of Woman as Other dominated European culture, keeping "woman" entrapped in myths which robbed her of her independent being and value. James Baldwin insisted that *all* culture was politically significant, and described the complexity of living with integrity as a Black person, an artist in a white-dominated culture, whether as an Afro-American growing up in Harlem, U.S.A., or as an African in a country emerging from a history of colonialism. He also alluded to "that as yet unwritten history of the Negro woman"; and he wrote in 1954 in an essay on Gide that "when men [heterosexual or homosexual] can no longer love women they also cease to love or respect or trust each other, which makes their isolation complete." And he was the first writer I read who suggested that racism was poisonous to white as well as destructive to Black people.

The idea of freedom—so much invoked during World War II—had become pretty abstract politically in the fifties. Freedom—then as now—was supposed to be what the Western democracies believed in and the "Iron Curtain" Soviet-bloc countries were deprived of. The existentialist philosophers who were beginning to be read and discussed among young American intellectuals spoke of freedom as something connected with revolt. But in reading de Beauvoir and Baldwin, I began to taste the concrete reality of being unfree, how continuous and permeating and corrosive a condition it is, and how it is maintained through culture as much as through the use of force.

I am telling you this from a backward perspective, from

where I stand now. At the time I could not have summed up the effect these writers had on me. I only knew that I was reading them with the same passion and need that I brought to poetry, that they were beginning to penetrate my life; I was beginning to feel as never before that I had some foothold, some way of seeing, which helped me to ask the questions I needed to ask.

But there were many voices then, as there are now, warning the North American artist against "mixing politics with art." I have been trying to retrace, to delineate, these arguments, which carry no weight for me now because I recognize them as the political declarations of privilege. There is the falsely mystical view of art that assumes a kind of supernatural inspiration, a possession by universal forces unrelated to questions of power and privilege or the artist's relation to bread and blood. In this view, the channel of art can only become clogged and misdirected by the artist's concern with merely temporary and local disturbances. The song is higher than the struggle, and the artist must choose between politics—here defined as earth-bound factionalism, corrupt power struggles—and art, which exists on some transcendent plane. This view of literature has dominated literary criticism in England and America for nearly a century. In the fifties and early sixties there was much shaking of heads if an artist was found "meddling in politics"; art was mystical and universal, but the artist was also, apparently, irresponsible and emotional and politically naïve.

In North America, moreover, "politics" is mostly a dirty word, associated with low-level wheeling and dealing, with manipulation. (There is nothing North Americans seem to fear so much as manipulation, probably because at some level we know that we belong to a deeply manipulative system.) "Politics" also suggested, certainly in the fifties, the Red Menace, Jewish plots, spies, malcontents conspiring to overthrow de-

mocracy, "outside agitators" stirring up perfectly contented
Black and/or working people. Such activities were dangerous
and punishable, and in the McCarthy era there was a great deal
of fear abroad. The writer Meridel LeSueur was blacklisted,
hounded by the FBI, her books banned; she was dismissed
from job after job—teaching, waitressing—because the FBI
intimidated her students and employers. A daughter of Tillie
Olsen recalls going with her mother in the 1950s to the Salva-
tion Army to buy heavy winter clothes because the family had
reason to believe that Leftists in the San Francisco Bay Area
would be rounded up and taken to detention camps farther
north. These are merely two examples of politically committed
writers who did survive that particular repression—many never
recovered from it.

Perhaps many white North Americans fear an overtly politi-
cal art because it might persuade us emotionally of what we
think we are "rationally" against; it might get to us on a level
we have lost touch with, undermine the safety we have built
for ourselves, remind us of what is better left forgotten. This
fear attributes real power to the voices of passion and of poetry
which connect us with all that is not simply white chauvinist
/male supremacist/straight/puritanical—with what is "dark,"
"effeminate," "inverted," "primitive," "volatile," "sinister."
Yet we are told that political poetry, for example, is doomed
to grind down into mere rhetoric and jargon, to become one-
dimensional, simplistic, vituperative; that in writing "protest
literature"—that is, writing from a perspective which may not
be male, or white, or heterosexual, or middle-class—we sac-
rifice the "universal"; that in writing of injustice we are limit-
ing our scope, "grinding a political axe." So political poetry is
suspected of immense subversive power, yet accused of being,
by definition, bad writing, impotent, lacking in breadth. No
wonder if the North American poet finds herself or himself

slightly crazed by the double messages.

By 1956, I had begun dating each of my poems by year. I did this because I was finished with the idea of a poem as a single, encapsulated event, a work of art complete in itself; I knew my life was changing, my work was changing, and I needed to indicate to readers my sense of being engaged in a long, continuing process. It seems to me now that this was an oblique political statement—a rejection of the dominant critical idea that the poem's text should be read as separate from the poet's everyday life in the world. It was a declaration that placed poetry in a historical continuity, not above or outside history.

In my own case, as soon as I published—in 1963—a book of poems which was informed by any conscious sexual politics, I was told, in print, that this work was "bitter," "personal"; that I had sacrificed the sweetly flowing measures of my earlier books for a ragged line and a coarsened voice. It took me a long time not to hear those voices internally whenever I picked up my pen. But I was writing at the beginning of a decade of political revolt and hope and activism. The external conditions for becoming a consciously, self-affirmingly political poet were there, as they had not been when I had begun to publish a decade earlier. Out of the Black Civil Rights movement, amid the marches and sit-ins in the streets and on campuses, a new generation of Black writers began to speak—and older generations to be reprinted and reread; poetry readings were infused with the spirit of collective rage and hope. As part of the movement against United States militarism and imperialism, white poets also were writing and reading aloud poems addressing the war in Southeast Asia. In many of these poems you sensed the poet's desperation in trying to encompass in words the reality of napalm, the "pacification" of villages, trying to make vivid in poetry what seemed to have minimal effect when shown on television. But there was little location of the self, the poet's own identity as a man or woman. As I wrote in another connection, "The enemy is always outside the self, the struggle somewhere else." I had—perhaps through reading de Beauvoir and Baldwin—some nascent idea that "Vietnam and the lovers' bed," as I phrased it then, were connected; I found myself, in the late sixties, trying to describe those relations in poetry. Even before I called myself a feminist or a lesbian, I felt driven—for my own sanity—to bring together in my poems the political world "out there"—the world of children dynamited or napalmed, of the urban ghetto and militarist violence, and the supposedly private, lyrical world of sex and of male/female relationships.

I began teaching in an urban subway college, in a program intended to compensate ghetto students for the inadequacy of the city's public schools. Among staff and students, and in the larger academic community, there were continual debates over the worth and even the linguistic existence of Black English, the expressive limits and social uses of Standard English—the politics of language. As a poet, I had learned much about both the value and the constraints of convention: the reassurances of traditional structures and the necessity to break from them in recognition of new experience. I felt more and more urgently the dynamic between poetry as language and poetry as a kind of action, probing, burning, stripping, placing itself in dialogue with others out beyond the individual self.

By the end of the 1960s an autonomous movement of women was declaring that "the personal is political." That statement was necessary because in other political movements of that decade the power relation of men to women, the question of women's roles and men's roles, had been dismissed—often contemptuously—as the sphere of personal life. Sex itself was not seen as political, except for interracial sex. Women were now talking about domination, not just in terms of economic exploitation, militarism, colonialism, imperialism, but within the family, in marriage, in child rearing, in the heterosexual act itself. Breaking the mental barrier that separated private from public life felt in itself like an enormous surge toward liberation. For a woman thus engaged, every aspect of her life was on the line. We began naming and acting on issues we had been told were trivial, unworthy of mention: rape by husbands or lovers; the boss's hand groping the employee's breast; the woman beaten in her home with no place to go; the woman sterilized when she sought an abortion; the lesbian penalized for her private life by loss of her child, her lease, her job. We pointed out that women's unpaid work in the home is central to every economy, capitalist or socialist. And in the crossover between personal and political, we were also pushing at the limits of experience reflected in literature, certainly in poetry.

To write directly and overtly as a woman, out of a woman's body and experience, to take women's existence seriously as theme and source for art, was something I had been hungering to do, needing to do, all my writing life. It placed me nakedly face to face with both terror and anger; it did indeed *imply the breakdown of the world as I had always known it, the end of safety,* to paraphrase Baldwin again. But it released tremendous energy in me, as in many other women, to have that way of writing affirmed and validated in a growing political community. I felt for the first time the closing of the gap between poet and woman.

Women have understood that we needed an art of our own: to remind us of our history and what we might be; to show us our true faces—all of them, including the unacceptable; to speak of what has been muffled in code or silence; to make concrete the values our movement was bringing forth out of consciousness raising, speakouts, and activism. But we were—

and are—living and writing not only within a women's commu-
nity. We are trying to build a political and cultural movement
in the heart of capitalism, in a country where racism assumes
every form of physical, institutional, and psychic violence, and
in which more than one person in seven lives below the poverty
line. The United States feminist movement is rooted in the
United States, a nation with a particular history of hostility
both to art and to socialism, where art has been encapsulated
as a commodity, a salable artifact, something to be taught in
MFA programs, that requires a special staff of "arts administra-
tors"; something you "gotta have" without exactly knowing
why. As a lesbian-feminist poet and writer, I need to under-
stand how this *location* affects me, along with the realities of
blood and bread within this nation.

"As a woman I have no country. As a woman I want no
country. As a woman my country is the whole world." These
words, written by Virginia Woolf in her feminist and anti-
fascist book *Three Guineas,* we dare not take out of context to
justify a false transcendence, an irresponsibility toward the
cultures and geopolitical regions in which we are rooted. Woolf
was attacking—as a feminist—patriotism, nationalism, the val-
ues of the British patriarchal establishment for which so many
wars have been fought all over the world. Her feminism led her
by the end of her life to anti-imperialism. As women, I think
it essential that we admit and explore our cultural identities,
our national identities, even as we reject the patriotism, jing-
oism, nationalism offered to us as "the American way of life."
Perhaps the most arrogant and malevolent delusion of North
American power—of white Western power—has been the de-
lusion of destiny, that white is at the center, that white is
endowed with some right or mission to judge and ransack and
assimilate and destroy the values of other peoples. As a white
feminist artist in the United States, I do not want to perpetuate
that chauvinism, but I still have to struggle with its pervasive-

ness in culture, its residues in myself.

Working as I do in the context of a movement in which artists are encouraged to address political and ethical questions, I have felt released to a large degree from the old separation of art from politics. But the presence of that separation "out there" in North American life is one of many impoverishing forces of capitalist patriarchy. I began to sense what it might be to live, and to write poetry, as a woman, in a society which took seriously the necessity for poetry, when I read Margaret Randall's anthology of contemporary Cuban women poets *Breaking the Silences*. This book had a powerful effect on me —the consistently high level of poetry, the diversity of voices, the sense of the poets' connections with world and community, and, in their individual statements, the affirmation of an organic relation between poetry and social transformation:

Things move so much around you.
Even your country has changed. You yourself have
changed it.

And the soul, will it change? You must change it.
Who will tell you otherwise?
Will it be a desolate journey?
Will it be tangible, languid
without a hint of violence?
As long as you are the person you are today
being yesterday's person as well,
you will be tomorrow's . . .
the one who lives and dies
to live like this.[2]

It was partly because of that book that I went to Nicaragua. I seized the opportunity when it arose, not because I thought

2. Nancy Morejón, "Elogia de la Dialéctica," in *Breaking the Silences: Twentieth Century Poetry by Cuban Women,* ed. Margaret Randall (1982, Pulp Press, Box 3868 MPO, Vancouver, Canada V6B 3Z3).

that everyone would be a poet, but because I had been feeling more and more ill informed, betrayed by the coverage of Central America in the United States media. I wanted to know what the Sandinistas believed they stood for, what directions they wanted to take in their very young, imperiled revolution. But I also wanted to get a sense of what art might mean in a society committed to values other than profit and consumerism. What was constantly and tellingly manifested was a *belief* in art, not as commodity, not as luxury, not as suspect activity, but as a precious resource to be made available to all, one necessity for the rebuilding of a scarred, impoverished, and still-bleeding country. And returning home I had to ask myself: What happens to the heart of the artist, here in North America? What toll is taken of art when it is separated from the social fabric? How is art curbed, how are we made to feel useless and helpless, in a system which so depends on our alienation?

Alienation—not just from the world of material conditions, of power to make things happen or stop happening. Alienation from our own roots, whatever they are, the memories, dreams, stories, the language, history, the sacred materials of art. In *A Gathering of Spirit,* an anthology of writing and art by North American Indian women, a poem by the Chicana/American Indian poet Anita Valerio reasserts the claim to a complex historical and cultural identity, the selves who are both of the past and of tomorrow:

> There is the cab driver root and elevator
> root, there is the water
> root of lies   The root of speech hidden in the secretary's
> marinated tongue   There is the ocean
> root and seeing
> root, heart and belly root, antelope
> roots hidden in hills   There is the root
> of the billy club/beginning with electric drums . . .

               root of hunters   smoky
     ascensions into heaven   trails
             beat out of ice   There is the root
     of homecoming   The house my grandfather built first   I see
     him   standing in his black
     hat beating the snake with a stick
             There is the root shaped
     by spirits speaking
     in the lodge   There is the root you don't
     want to hear and the one that hides
     from you under the couch. . . .

             Root of teeth and
     the nape of the goat   oranges,   fog
     written on a camera   There is the carrot owl hunting
     for her hat in the wind   moccasins
                                     of the blue deer
         flashing
     in the doorknob. . . .
             There is the root of sex eating
     pound cake in the kitchen   crumbs
                                     crumbs
                                         alibis
     crumbs
     a convict astroprojects   She is
     picking up her torches, picking up her psalms, her
     necklaces[3]

     I write in full knowledge that the majority of the world's
     illiterates are women, that I live in a technologically advanced
     country where 40 percent of the people can barely read and 20
     percent are functionally illiterate.[4] I believe that these facts are
     directly connected to the fragmentations I suffer in myself,
     that we are all in this together. Because I can write at all—and

     3. Anita Valerio, "I Am Listening: A Lyric of Roots," in *A Gathering of Spirit,
     Sinister Wisdom* 22/23 (1983, ed. Beth Brant): 212–213.
     4. See p. 4, n. 1, and p. 161, n. 1, above.

I think of all the ways women especially have been prevented from writing—because my words are read and taken seriously, because I see my work as part of something larger than my own life or the history of literature, I feel a responsibility to keep searching for teachers who can help me widen and deepen the sources and examine the ego that speaks in my poems—not for political "correctness," but for ignorance, solipsism, laziness, dishonesty, automatic writing. I look everywhere for signs of that fusion I have glimpsed in the women's movement, and most recently in Nicaragua. I turn to Toni Cade Bambara's *The Salt Eaters* or Ama Ata Aidoo's *Our Sister Killjoy* or James Baldwin's *Just above My Head;* to paintings by Frida Kahlo or Jacob Lawrence; to poems by Dionne Brand or Judy Grahn or Audre Lorde or Nancy Morejón; to the music of Nina Simone or Mary Watkins. This kind of art—like the art of so many others uncanonized in the dominant culture—is not produced as a commodity, but as part of a long conversation with the elders and with the future. (And, yes, I do live and work believing in a future.) Such artists draw on a tradition in which political struggle and spiritual continuity are meshed. Nothing need be lost, no beauty sacrificed. The heart does not turn to a stone.

The Soul of a Women's College (1984)

I have been asked to speak to you once again on the birthday
of Susan B. Anthony. One of Anthony's late great projects was
the opening of the University of Rochester, New York, to
women students. When the trustees of that institution de-
manded that $100,000 be raised as the price of women's admis-
sion, she personally spearheaded a fund-raising campaign. In
the last several days before the appointed time ran out, she
traveled the length and breadth of the city, demanding contri-
butions from every wealthy man and woman she knew, insist-
ing that the chance must not be lost. She pledged her own life
insurance for the last $2,000 and in her diary was finally able
to write, "They let the girls in. There was no alternative."

This was less than a century ago, in 1891. In 1858, Ellen
Browning Scripps had become one of the first women college
students in the country, at a female seminary grudgingly
opened by Knox College, which granted women neither di-
plomas nor degrees. Seventy-nine years later and only thirty-six
years after Rochester University "let the girls in," Ellen Scripps
made possible the founding of Scripps College. I am not going

Lecture given at Scripps College, Claremont, California, February 15, 1984.

to attempt here an overview of higher education for women in this country. Such a history would have to include the earliest co-educational land-grant colleges; the founding of elite women's colleges in the Northeast and Southeast; the Black colleges; the struggles of women to obtain admission to graduate and professional schools; the debates as to whether women should be prepared for marriage and motherhood, with emphasis on domestic economy, child psychology, and the arts as a measure of good taste, or for traditionally female jobs such as teaching, nursing, social service; whether the course of study for women should be the same as that traditionally offered men of the same class. Within and outside women's colleges, these debates have continued, along with an underlying, if sometimes unspoken, question: Is a women's college a place for women to be protected or a place for women's empowerment? At different times and in different places, different answers have been given, sometimes in statements of purpose, sometimes vividly and personally conveyed by those who guide and teach—women as remarkable and as dissimilar as Mary McLeod Bethune, founder of what is now Bethune-Cookman College, which began as the Daytona Industrial and Normal School for Girls, and M. Carey Thomas, early president of Bryn Mawr. And the dynamic of those questions is very much with us today. What is a women's college for? Why here and not somewhere else? What does it mean to educate women?

The thoughts I am going to share with you are the thoughts of a caring outsider. I am the graduate of a women's college —a separate enclave of women students in a male university. I have taught in women's colleges and Women's Studies programs as well as in feminist institutions, and much of my teaching life has been centered on women's education. But I do not really belong to academia in the sense of carrying the year-after-year continuity of an institution as my responsibility.

Some of you have experience of that responsibility, with all its burdens and opportunities, which I have never had. And so these remarks are not intended to be prescriptive, but simply suggestive. I would like to induce a kind of *wishful thinking,* first of all. "Wishful thinking" has a bad name—it suggests self-delusion, daydreaming without foundations. But by "wishful thinking" I mean what Martin Buber called "imagining the real"—placing our desires out before us and then seeing how to go about making them possible. Feminism has always been shaped and fired by the question *How can things be other than they are? What if . . . ?* It is this kind of thinking that I hope you will engage in with me tonight.

First, a brief look at what is. We are here in the United States in 1984. Whether or not Reagan is defeated in November, the social fabric of the United States will be feeling for a long time the effects of his administration's policies—its military excesses, its war against the poor, its cutbacks on health, on education, on environmental safety, on freedom of information. In four years, it is possible to undo and unmake a great deal, and some losses can never be made up. I have been thinking that after a war it is usual to raise plaques in local communities, memorials with the names of the dead who are officially accounted for and mourned. But there is no such list of the children and women and men who have been and are being lost to us through malnutrition, substandard schooling, illegal and incompetent abortions, drugs, a health-care system which works, if at all, only for the privileged; through industrial poisoning, unregulated public squalor; through deprivation of hope. And there is no way of measuring the damage to a society when a whole texture of humanity is kept from realizing its own power, when the woman architect who might have reinvented our cities sits barely literate in a semilegal sweatshop on the Texas-Mexican border, when women who should be founding colleges must work their entire lives as domestics, when poets and community leaders and visionaries and ordinary people with heart and wit, with a tale to tell, a hand that can paint or carve, are dying from uranium-contaminated water and the dumping of carcinogenic wastes. I am talking about the loss, not just to certain communities, but to all of us—deliberate wasting of lives, not natural disaster. And we know it is the women in every family and community who take the weight of trying to make do, repair, console. A women's college needs consciously to define itself against this background.

At this time and in this place, the function of educational institutions is the preparation of certain kinds of people to occupy certain places in the work force, and in the division of private from public life. (When I say "function," I don't mean idealistic statements of principle; I mean what actually happens.) White males are primarily guided toward and trained for the upper-level professional class; white males, some white females, and a very small group of men and women of color toward the middle-level professional class. People of color and poor white females receive the lowest levels of education and are shunted as cheap labor toward lower-paying, unskilled, and service jobs, and, of course, into the armed forces, which actually advertise themselves as educational institutions.

This American educational system is partially responsible for the fact that in a period of economic crisis like the present, most of the "newly poor" are women, most families living below the poverty line are headed by minority women, most of the impoverished old are women, and it is women whose unpaid labor in the home constitutes a second job unrecompensed as work.

It is difficult to keep these stark facts foremost in our thinking as we move through the serene, almost ethereal beauty of the Claremont campuses and the streets around them. But they stand as realities, challenging the myth that with a white woman Supreme Court justice, a Black Miss America, and a white woman astronaut, women are now equal participants in an American society with open opportunities for all. This has never been a society with open opportunities for all, and women are very selectively invited to participate.

What does all this mean for the students, the faculty, the administrators of a women's college, let alone for the employees whose names don't even get into the catalogue?

Is a women's college meant to prepare women for life? For what kind of life? For the security-card condominium, or the barrio, or the underground fallout shelter? Is it meant to instill the white, male, Western tradition of knowledge and values or something quite different? Is it meant to teach obedience or dissatisfaction? Is it conceived as a kind of convent, a relief and escape from the heterosexual pressures of high school, or is it to be an experience in female community as a positive and an empowering value in itself? Is a women's college, by implication, feminist? Should it be feminist? What would this mean?

Preparing for this evening, I wanted to ground myself in the history of this place, at least to some extent, and to know what spirit lay behind its creation. I had noted the name of Ellen Browning Scripps inscribed on several walls and had vaguely assumed—I wonder why?—that she was the wife of the man who had founded the Scripps-Howard newspaper empire. It was interesting to learn that in fact she had never married and had herself co-founded, with her brothers, the *Detroit News* and the *Cleveland Press,* forerunners of that empire. It was impressive to see the breadth of her interests as evidenced by the range of her generosity, including her gifts to science. It was thought-provoking to find that she, like so many women of purpose and achievement, had lived for thirty years with another woman, alluded to in a biographical sketch only once as Miss Gardner but described as a "vigilant companion." I wondered about Miss Gardner and about the conversations the two women might have had about the founding of a women's college, what Miss Gardner's part was in Ellen Scripps's vision, in the way that two long-time companions can turn and bestir each others' thinking.

I thought of the fact that although Ellen Scripps was never to walk on this campus, she followed the life of the new college in detail, met with students into her late nineties, and died a century old. I have wished for more time to go and read her papers, to have more than the taste of her mind that is given us by the lively sample from her travel letters discovered and edited by Dorothy Drake. It is difficult, from the inscriptions on college walls, to gain a three-dimensional picture of a human being. Yet, irresistibly, I have found myself in a running conversation with Ellen Scripps, based on those letters.

For example, she says to me: "You know, I always wanted to be a doctor. But women were not admitted to medical schools back then."

And I say, "What are the professions you think women should be trained to enter?"

"Oh, my dear," she says, "what really interests them, of course. To be useful—as a scientist, as a lawmaker, to study society and make it better. Of course, women have certain interests that are more natural to their sex."

"What are those?" I ask.

"Nursing, of course, and medicine, teaching, dietetics, the science of child rearing."

I ask: "Well, but, are you sure those are more natural for women than studying life under the ocean, or the gathering and publishing of news, or interpreting the laws? Was physics unnatural for the young Marie Skłodowska Curie or ecology for Rachel Carson? How can a woman *know* what really interests her when she is told that some things are less natural to her than others?"

"My dear," she says, "the important thing is that a woman work usefully in the world, that she have an education that will prepare her to do so. There's not much point in preparing her for professions which are closed to her. But she should have her mind opened up to all kinds of possibilities."

"It seems to me you're saying that a women's college should adapt its curriculum to the existing premises about women in the society, and at the same time you're saying that it should open women's minds to all kinds of possibilities. Do you think a traditional liberal-arts curriculum can do that second thing?"

"Let me tell you about my college education," she says. "Knox College let us in, but they kept us in separate classrooms, and we were called the Knox Female Seminary. We weren't allowed to study certain courses or even certain authors like Euripides. We had a lot of literature of the more ladylike sort, and French and Latin, a bit; no real mathematics, philosophy, or modern history. When I was thinking about a women's college, I felt most passionately that it should offer a course of study which would not condescend to the students' minds, which would recognize that women can learn anything men can learn."

"And yet," I persist, "in the earliest statement of Scripps's educational policy, there's a lot about training in homemaking and business education, 'with emphasis on investing and the care of investments' and also about teaching, health service, home administration. . . . I can see that that policy changed, but it seems that originally the idea of Scripps as a women's college was a college to help train women in so-called womanly professions."

"You do know," says Ellen Scripps, "that I wasn't the sole architect of the educational policy. For better or for worse, there were always the trustees."

"When you went to Knox Female Seminary," I say, "it was extremely important for you as a woman to be getting any further education at all. By the time you founded Scripps—I know you don't like that word, but at all events Scripps came into being through you—you were determined that women should not just have one foot in higher education, but should be equal sharers in that great world of ideas which you had absorbed partly on your own, through your travels, your work, your wide reading, your interest in human affairs. But you were also a suffragist and a defender of those who were jailed for unpopular ideas—a believer in freedom of speech. How did you feel about the way that traditional liberal-arts curriculum, what's called 'the humanities,' had left women out almost completely? Did you think it was enough to admit women into the old fields of study? Don't you think that the fields of study themselves have to change?"

"I knew you were going to ask me that," she says. "So far I have answered your questions because they had to do with things that were being discussed and happening in my lifetime. Don't you know that there's a strict rule about interviewing the dead, that you mustn't ask us questions which come out of *your* time frame? There is just too much danger of our being misquoted. But I'll tell you something. Just at the end, it came to me that Scripps College, which I had never seen but whose people and issues I knew well, was still incomplete, not in terms of buildings or programs, but that she had not yet gained her soul. I began to feel how much more meaning there was to a women's college than even I had ever realized. I had cared a lot about the quality of life for women on a campus with men; I had wanted a place which women would feel was theirs. And I wondered—so late—why I had felt that pressing need. I think that it came from something I hadn't understood before, because my own life had been so fortunate in so many ways and so exceptional. That most of the world is not a women's place, but a women-negating place, and that women need a sense of what a women's place can be—not somewhere to retire to and be protected but to become empowered, go forth from, sure of their own value and integrity. I realized then that it meant not just having beautiful residence halls and gardens, but a soul. That's *my* word—I think today you feminists call it 'consciousness.' "

I have come to the end of my poetic license for this evening. But I'd like to throw out some final thoughts. For the poverty, the double workload, the social disempowerment of the vast majority of women to change, for anything to change beyond the careers of a privileged few, we have to think critically in terms of the entire society—the sacredness of profit, the expendability of human beings. I am thinking how we can educate women for a world in which social and sexual and cultural differences will be respected, where the white, male, Western perspective will be one of many, and not the predominant one. For I am not alone in believing that this is the only kind of human society that will survive. I am thinking how we educate women to respect themselves and each other and refuse to countenance disrespect. One source of respect is memory—the understanding of where we have come from and who we have been—a core curriculum, let us say, of women's history, thought, political roles, labor, art, not just those of white women, Western women, but a deeper, richer, more diverse kind of memory. That no woman should leave a women's college ignorant of that history. I am thinking that for this, more is needed than reading and writing. Visual art throughout the campus is needed, from many cultures, not restricted to a museum or classroom, but in the form of posters, murals, sculpture, photographs, films, images that depict the physical and spiritual facts of many kinds of women's lives: not only Euro-American but native American, Asian, African, Sephardic, Islamic, Latin, Aboriginal. If women are to learn computer science, I am thinking of studies and lectures on the relation of women and computers, on the political and economic implications for the female workers handling the chips on the assembly lines of Southeast Asia. If women are to be learning physics and biochemistry, let them also have critical seminars on scientific revolutions, the connections between science and industry and government, and what admission to *that* world means to the "girls" who are "let in." I am thinking of a history of science taught from a gendered perspective, of an economics taught from the perspective of women's work. I am thinking that a study of decision making and group process under different conditions and traditions might be as important for a young woman as a creative-writing workshop—teaching her not mere "assertiveness," but old and new ways of resolving conflict, of coalition building, of collective participation. I am thinking of an institute for already active women artists and scholars who would also interact with students. I am thinking how the conscious preparation of women for participation would involve students and teachers in cross-cultural, multiracial studies and in the study of the many liberation movements in which women have played leading roles. How the "untrammeled discussion" which Ellen Scripps profoundly believed in would be encouraged and facilitated, and no lesbian need feel invisible nor be treated as threat. How the question *What does this mean for women?* would be an expected and natural part of any discussion. I am thinking how a women's college, fully conscious of its own meaning, might become the vital pulse, the intellectual nerve center, the critical cutting edge of a cluster of colleges like this one.

Invisibility in Academe
(1984)

The history of North American lesbians under white domination begins with the death penalty prescribed for lesbians in 1656 in New Haven, Connecticut. Three hundred years later, in the 1950s, lesbians were being beaten in the city streets, committed to mental institutions, forced to undergo psychosurgery, often at their parents' instigation. Thirty years after that, in the mid-1980s, despite the struggles and visions of both the Women's Liberation movement and the gay liberation movement, lesbians are still being assaulted in the streets—during the past year in the streets of Northampton, Massachusetts, the site of a women's college near which I live. Lesbians are still being forced to endure behavior modification and medical punishment, are still banished from families, are rejected by our ethnic, racial, and religious communities, must pretend to be heterosexual in order to hold jobs, have custody of their children, rent apartments, publicly represent a larger community.

Beside all this, invisibility may seem a small price to pay (as in "All we ask is that you keep your private life private" or "Just

Talk given at the Scripps College Conference, Claremont, California, 1984.

don't use the word"). But invisibility is a dangerous and painful condition, and lesbians are not the only people to know it. When those who have power to name and to socially construct reality choose not to see you or hear you, whether you are dark-skinned, old, disabled, female, or speak with a different accent or dialect than theirs, when someone with the authority of a teacher, say, describes the world and you are not in it, there is a moment of psychic disequilibrium, as if you looked into a mirror and saw nothing. Yet you know you exist and others like you, that this is a game with mirrors. It takes some strength of soul—and not just individual strength, but collective understanding—to resist this void, this nonbeing, into which you are thrust, and to stand up, demanding to be seen and heard. And to make yourself visible, to claim that your experience is just as real and normative as any other, as "moral and ordinary" in the words of historian Blanche Cook, can mean making yourself vulnerable. But at least you are not doing the oppressor's work, building your own closet. It is important to me to remember that in the nineteenth century, women—all women —were forbidden by law to speak in public meetings. Society depended on their muteness. But some, and then more and more, refused to be mute and spoke up. Without them, we would not even be here today.

I have been for ten years a very public and visible lesbian. I have been identified as a lesbian in print both by myself and others; I have worked in the lesbian-feminist movement. Here in Claremont, where I have been received with much warmth and hospitality, I have often felt invisible as a lesbian. I have felt my identity as a feminist threatening to some, welcome to others; but my identity as a lesbian is something that many people would prefer not to know about. And this experience has reminded me of what I should never have let myself forget: that invisibility is not just a matter of being told to keep your private life private; it's the attempt to fragment you, to prevent you from integrating love and work and feelings and ideas, with the empowerment that that can bring.

I'm not talking only about this community. There are many places, including Women's Studies programs, where this fragmentation goes on. The basis for dialogue and discussion remains heterosexual, while perhaps a section of a reading list or a single class period is supposed to "include" lesbian experience and thought. In an almost identical way, the experience and thought of women of color is relegated to a special section, added as an afterthought, while the central discourse remains unrelentingly white, usually middle-class in its assumptions and priorities. The name of the second set of blinders is racism; of the first, heterosexism. The Black political scientist Gloria I. Joseph, in a talk on "Third World Women and Feminism," has suggested that *homophobia* is an inaccurate term, implying a form of uncontrollable mental panic, and that *heterosexism* better describes what is really a deeply ingrained prejudice, comparable to racism, sexism, and classism—a political indoctrination which must be recognized as such and which can be re-educated.

I want to suggest that it is impossible for any woman growing up in a gendered society dominated by men to know what heterosexuality really means, both historically and in her individual life, so long as she is kept ignorant of the presence, the existence, the actuality of women who, diverse in so many ways, have centered their emotional and erotic lives on women. A young woman entering her twenties in a blur of stereotypes and taboos, with a vague sense of anxiety centering around the word *lesbian,* is ill equipped to think about herself, her feelings, her options, her relations with men *or* women. This ignorance and anxiety, which affects lesbians and heterosexually identified women alike, this silence, this absence of a whole population, this invisibility, is disempowering for all women. It is not only lesbian students who should be calling for a recognition of their history and presence in the world; it is *all* women who want a more accurate map of the way social relations have been and are, as they try to imagine what might be.

I think that those of us who are lesbians here sense that there are people who want to meet us in our wholeness instead of fragments, and others who do not want to know, who run away, who want us to be quiet, who will use all kinds of indirect and genteel means to keep us that way, including the charge that we never talk about anything else. I believe there is a critical mass in this community—not only lesbians—who recognize the intellectual and moral sterility of heterosexism. I hope that we can find ways of speaking with each other that will strengthen a collective understanding that will keep discussion continuing long after this conference is over.

If Not with Others, How? (1985)

I have been reflecting on what feels so familiar about all this: to identify actively as a woman and ask what that means; to identify actively as a Jew and ask what that means. It is feminist politics—the efforts of women trying to work together as women across sexual, class, racial, ethnic, and other lines—that have pushed me to look at the starved Jew in myself; finally, to seek a path to that Jewishness still unsatisfied, still trying to define its true homeland, still untamed and unsuburbanized, still wandering in the wilderness. Over and over, the work of Jewish feminists has inspired and challenged me to educate myself, culturally and politically and spiritually, from Jewish sources, to cast myself into the ancient and turbulent river of disputation which is Jewish culture.

Jews, like women, exist everywhere, our existence often veiled by history; we have been "the Jewish question" or "the woman question" at the margins of Leftist politics, while Right Wing repressions have always zeroed in on us. We have—

Excerpted from a keynote address for the New Jewish Agenda National Convention, Ann Arbor, Michigan, July 1985. This excerpt was first published in Genesis 2: An Independent Voice for Jewish Renewal *(February–March 1986).*

women and Jews—been the targets of biological determinism and persistent physical violence. We have been stereotyped both viciously and sentimentally by others and have often taken these stereotypes into ourselves. Of course, the two groups interface: women are Jews, and Jews are women; but what this means for the Jewish vision, we are only beginning to ask. We exist everywhere under laws we did not make; speaking a multitude of languages; excluded by law and custom from certain spaces, functions, resources associated with power; often accused of wielding too much power, of wielding dark and devious powers. Like Black and other dark-skinned people, Jews and women have haunted white Western thought as Other, as fantasy, as projected obsession.

My hope is that the movement we are building can further the conscious work of turning Otherness into a keen lens of empathy, that we can bring into being a politics based on concrete, heartfelt understanding of what it means to be Other. We are women and men, *Mischlings* (of mixed parentage) and the sons and daughters of rabbis, Holocaust survivors, freedom fighters, teachers, middle- and working-class Jews. We are gay and straight and bisexual, older and younger, differently able and temporarily able-bodied; and we share an unquenched hope for the survival and sanity of the human community. Believing that no single people can survive being only for itself, we want a base from which to act on our hope.

I feel proud to be identified as a Jew among Jews, not simply a progressive among progressives, a feminist among feminists. And I ask myself, What does that mean? What is this pride in tribe, family, culture, heritage? Is it a feeling of being better than those outside the tribe? The medieval philosopher Judah ha-Levi claimed a hierarchy of all species, places on earth, races, families, and even languages. In this hierarchy, the land, language, and people of Israel are naturally superior to all others. As a woman, I reject all such hierarchies.

Then is pride merely a cloak I pull around me in the face of anti-Semitism, in the face of the contempt and suspicion of others? Do I invoke pride as a shield against my enemies, or do I find its sources deeper in my being, where I define myself for myself?

Difficult questions for any people who for centuries have met with derogation of identity. Pride is often born in the place where we refuse to be victims, where we experience our own humanity under pressure, where we understand that we are not the hateful projections of others but intrinsically ourselves. Where does this take us? It helps us fight for survival, first of all, because we know, from somewhere, we deserve to survive. "I am not an inferior life form" becomes "There is sacred life, energy, plenitude in me and in those like me you are trying to destroy." And if, in the example of others like me, I learn not only survival but the plenitude of life, if I feel linked by a texture of values, history, words, passions to people long dead or whom I have never met, if I celebrate these linkages, is this what I mean by pride? Or am I really talking about love?

Pride is a tricky, glorious, double-edged feeling. I don't feel proud of everything Jews have done or thought, nor of everything women have done or thought. The poet Irena Klepfisz has confronted in her long poem "Bashert" the question of sorting out a legacy without spurning any of it, a legacy that includes both courage and ardor, and the shrinking of the soul under oppression, the damages suffered. In any one like me, I have to see mirrored my own shrinkings of soul, my own damages.

Yet I must make my choices, take my positions according to my conscience and vision now. To separate from parts of a legacy in a conscious, loving, and responsible way in order to say "This is frayed and needs repair; that no longer serves us;

this is still vital and usable" is not to spurn tradition, but to take it very seriously. Those who refuse to make these distinctions —and making distinctions has been a very Jewish preoccupation—those who suppress criticism of the Jewish legacy suppress further creation.

As an American Jew, I fear the extent to which both Americans and Israelis, in their national consciousness, are captives of denial. Denial, first, of the existence of the peoples who, in the creation of both nations, have been swept aside, their communities destroyed, pushed into reservations and camps, traumatized by superior might calling itself destiny. I fear that this denial, this unaccountability for acts which are still continuing, is a deep infection in the collective life and conscience of both nations.

America wants to forget the past, and the past in the present; and one result of that was Bitburg. Israeli denial is different. Years ago, I remember seeing, with great emotion, on the old Jerusalem–Tel Aviv road, rusted tanks left from the 1948 war, on one of which was painted "If I forget thee, O Jerusalem . . . " But Palestinian memory has been violently obliterated. I fear for the kind of "moral autism" (Amos Oz's phrase) out of which both the United States and Israel, in their respective capacities of power, have made decisions leading to physical carnage and to acute internal disequilibrium and suffering.

I say this here, knowing my words will be understood or at least not heard as anti-Semitism. But many of us have experienced a censorship in American Jewish communities, where dissent from official Israeli policies and actions is rebuked and Jewish critical introspection is silenced. "The armored and concluded mind" (Muriel Rukeyser's phrase)[1] is not what the Jewish mind has been overall. Torah itself is not

---

1. *The Collected Poems of Muriel Rukeyser* (New York: McGraw-Hill, 1978), p. 102.

a closed system; we have been a people unafraid of argument,
a people of many opinions. Our forebears were instructed to
commit suicide rather than idolatry; yet Israel has become a
kind of idol for many American Jews. Israel is not seen and
cared about as an unfinished human effort, harrowed and
flawed and full of gashes between dreams and realities, but as
an untouchable construct: The Place Where Jews Can Be Safe.
I think that the taboo on dissent among American Jews dam-
ages all Jews who, in the wake of the Holocaust and the birth
of a Jewish state, are trying to imagine a Jewish future and a
Jewish consciousness that does not stop with Hillel's first ques-
tion.[2]

The word *safe* has two distinct connotations: one, of a place
in which we can draw breath, rest from persecution or harass-
ment, bear witness, lick our wounds, feel compassion and love
around us rather than hostility or indifference. The safety of
the mother's lap for the bullied child, of the battered-women's
shelter, the door opened to us when we need a refuge. Safety
in this sense implies a place to gather our forces, a place to
move from, not a destination. But there is also the safety of the
"armored and concluded mind," the safety of the barricaded
door which will not open for the beleaguered Stranger, the
psychotic safety of the underground nuclear-bomb shelter, the
walled and guarded crime-proof condominium, the safety
bought with guns and money at no matter what cost, the safety
bought and sold at the cost of shutting up. And this safety
becomes a dead end in the mind and in the mapping of a life
or a collective vision. I want to say that though the longing for
safety has been kept awake in us by centuries of danger, mere
safety has not been the central obsession of the Jewish people.

2. "If I am not for myself, who will be for me?" See *Sayings of the Fathers, or Pirke
Aboth, the Hebrew text, with a New English Translation and a Commentary by the Very
Rev. Dr. Joseph H. Hertz* (New York: Behrman House, 1945), p. 25.

It has not been an ultimate destination. How to live in compassion, pursue justice, create a society in which "what is hateful to you, do not do to your neighbor," how to think, praise, celebrate life—these have been fundamental to Jewish vision. Even if strayed from, given lip service, even if in this vision Jewish women have remained Other, even if many Jews have acted on this vision as social reformists and radicals without realizing how Jewish—though not exclusively Jewish—a vision it is. And I don't believe that the Jewish genius has completed itself on this earth: I think it may be on the verge of a new, if often painful and disorienting, renascence.

All of us here live in two dissonant worlds. There is the world of this community and others like it in America: Jewish and gentile, men and women, Black and brown and red and yellow and white, old and young, educated in books and educated in what Tillie Olsen has named "the college of work," in poverty or in privilege—the communities of those who are trying to "turn the century," in Black activist musician Bernice Reagon's words.[3] In this world of vision and struggle, there is still myopia, division, anti-Semitism, racism, sexism, heterosexism. But there is also passion, and persistence, and memory, and the determination to build what we need, and the refusal to buy safety or comfort by shutting up. We affirm the diversity out of which we come, the clashes and pain we experience in trying to work together, the unglamorous ongoing labors of love and necessity.

And there is that other world, that America whose history is Disneyland, whose only legitimized passion is white male violence, whose people are starving for literal food and also for intangible sustenance they cannot always name, whose opiate

3. Bernice Reagon, "Turning the Century," in *Home Girls: A Black Feminist Anthology*, ed. Barbara Smith (New York: Kitchen Table/Women of Color Press, 1981), pp. 356–368.

is denial. As progressives, we live in this America, too, and it affects us. Even as we try to change it, it affects us. This America that has never mourned or desisted in or even acknowledged the original, deliberate, continuing genocide of the indigenous American people now called the Indians. This America that has never acknowledged or mourned or desisted in the ordinary, banal murderousness of its racism—murderous of the individuals and groups targeted by skin color, and murderous of the spiritual integrity of all of us.

As Jews, we have tried to comprehend the losses encompassed by the Holocaust, not just in terms of numbers or communities or families or individuals, but in terms of unknown potentialities—voices, visions, spiritual and ethical—of which we and the world are irreparably deprived. As American Jews, our losses are not from the Holocaust alone. We are citizens of a country deprived of the effective moral, ethical, and aesthetic visions of those whom white racism has tried to quench in both subtle and violent ways; whose capacity, nonetheless, to insist on their humanity, to persevere and resist, to educate their fellow citizens in political reality, to carry their "message for the world," as W. E. B. Du Bois called it, should be supported and celebrated by Jews everywhere.

For progressive American Jews, racism as it exists here in America, around and also within us, in the air we breathe, has both an ethical and a pragmatic urgency. We cannot continue to oppose the racism of Kahane and his like or of South African apartheid and take less oppositional stands on the malignancy of racism here where we live. The depth of the work we do depends on its rootedness—in our knowledge of who we are and also of where we are—a country which has used skin color as the prime motive for persecution and genocide, as Europe historically used religion. As Elly Bulkin indicates in a mind-stretching essay, "Hard Ground": "In terms of anti-Semitism and racism, a central problem is how to acknowledge their differences without contributing to the argument that one is important and the other is not, one is worthy of serious attention and the other is not."[4] It is difficult to move beyond these polarizations, but we are learning to do so and will, I believe, continue to help each other learn.

We must continue to insist that the concepts of Jewish survival and "what is good for the Jews" have an expanding, not a constricting, potential. I long to see the widest range of progressive issues defined as Jewish issues everywhere in this country. I long to see the breaking of encrustations of fear and caution, habits of thought engrained by centuries of endangerment and by the spiritual sterility of white mainstream America. I long to see Jewish energy, resources, passion, our capacity to celebrate life pouring into a gathering of thousands of American Jews toward "turning the century." I believe the potential is there; I long to see it stirred into glowing life. I believe we may be at the watershed for such a movement. And I would like to end by reading Hillel's three questions, which can never really be separated, and by adding a fourth, which is implicit in what we are doing:

> *If I am not for myself, who will be for me?*
> *If I am only for myself, what am I?*
> *If not now, when?*
>
> *If not with others, how?*

---

4. Elly Bulkin, "Hard Ground: Jewish Identity, Racism, and Anti-Semitism," in Elly Bulkin, M. B. Pratt, and B. Smith, *Yours in Struggle: Three Feminist Perspectives on Anti-Semitism and Racism* (Brooklyn, N.Y.: Long Haul, 1984; distributed by Firebrand Books, Ithaca, N.Y.).

Notes toward a Politics of Location (1984)

I am to speak these words in Europe, but I have been searching for them in the United States of America. A few years ago I would have spoken of the common oppression of women, the gathering movement of women around the globe, the hidden history of women's resistance and bonding, the failure of all previous politics to recognize the universal shadow of patriarchy, the belief that women now, in a time of rising consciousness and global emergency, may join across all national and cultural boundaries to create a society free of domination, in which "sexuality, politics, . . . work, . . . intimacy . . . thinking itself will be transformed."[1]

I would have spoken these words as a feminist who "happened" to be a white United States citizen, conscious of my government's proven capacity for violence and arrogance of power, but as self-separated from that government, quoting

Talk given at the First Summer School of Critical Semiotics, Conference on Women, Feminist Identity and Society in the 1980s, Utrecht, Holland, June 1, 1984. Different versions of this talk were given at Cornell University for the Women's Studies Research Seminar, and as the Burgess Lecture, Pacific Oaks College, Pasadena, California.
    1. Adrienne Rich, *Of Woman Born: Motherhood as Experience and Institution* (New York: W. W. Norton, 1976), p. 286.

without second thought Virginia Woolf's statement in *Three Guineas* that "as a woman I have no country. As a woman I want no country. As a woman my country is the whole world."

This is not what I come here to say in 1984. I come here with notes but without absolute conclusions. This is not a sign of loss of faith or hope. These notes are the marks of a struggle to keep moving, a struggle for accountability.

Beginning to write, then getting up. Stopped by the movements of a huge early bumblebee which has somehow gotten inside this house and is reeling, bumping, stunning itself against windowpanes and sills. I open the front door and speak to it, trying to attract it outside. It is looking for what it needs, just as I am, and, like me, it has gotten trapped in a place where it cannot fulfill its own life. I could open the jar of honey on the kitchen counter, and perhaps it would take honey from that jar; but its life process, its work, its mode of being cannot be fulfilled inside this house.

And I, too, have been bumping my way against glassy panes, falling half-stunned, gathering myself up and crawling, then again taking off, searching.

I don't hear the bumblebee any more, and I leave the front door. I sit down and pick up a secondhand, faintly annotated student copy of Marx's *The German Ideology*, which "happens" to be lying on the table.

I will speak these words in Europe, but I am having to search for them in the United States of North America. When I was ten or eleven, early in World War II, a girlfriend and I used to write each other letters which we addressed like this:

Adrienne Rich
14 Edgevale Road

Baltimore, Maryland
The United States of America
The Continent of North America
The Western Hemisphere
The Earth
The Solar System
The Universe

You could see your own house as a tiny fleck on an ever-widening landscape, or as the center of it all from which the circles expanded into the infinite unknown.

It is that question of feeling at the center that gnaws at me now. At the center of what?

As a woman I have a country; as a woman I cannot divest myself of that country merely by condemning its government or by saying three times "As a woman my country is the whole world." Tribal loyalties aside, and even if nation-states are now just pretexts used by multinational conglomerates to serve their interests, I need to understand how a place on the map is also a place in history within which as a woman, a Jew, a lesbian, a feminist I am created and trying to create.

Begin, though, not with a continent or a country or a house, but with the geography closest in—the body. Here at least I know I exist, that living human individual whom the young Marx called "the first premise of all human history."[2] But it was not as a Marxist that I turned to this place, back from philosophy and literature and science and theology in which I had looked for myself in vain. It was as a radical feminist.

The politics of pregnability and motherhood. The politics of orgasm. The politics of rape and incest, of abortion, birth

---

2. Karl Marx and Frederick Engels, *The German Ideology*, ed. C. J. Arthur (New York: International Publishers, 1970), p. 42.

control, forcible sterilization. Of prostitution and marital sex. Of what had been named sexual liberation. Of prescriptive heterosexuality. Of lesbian existence.

And Marxist feminists were often pioneers in this work. But for many women I knew, the need to begin with the female body—our own—was understood not as applying a Marxist principle *to* women, but as locating the grounds from which to speak with authority *as* women. Not to transcend this body, but to reclaim it. To reconnect our thinking and speaking with the body of this particular living human individual, a woman. Begin, we said, with the material, with matter, mma, madre, mutter, moeder, modder, etc., etc.

Begin with the material. Pick up again the long struggle against lofty and privileged abstraction. Perhaps this is the core of revolutionary process, whether it calls itself Marxist or Third World or feminist or all three. Long before the nineteenth century, the empirical witch of the European Middle Ages, trusting her senses, practicing her tried remedies against the anti-material, anti-sensuous, anti-empirical dogmas of the Church. Dying for that, by the millions. "A female-led peasant rebellion"?—in any event, a rebellion against the idolatry of pure ideas, the belief that ideas have a life of their own and float along above the heads of ordinary people—women, the poor, the uninitiated.[3]

Abstractions severed from the doings of living people, fed back to people as slogans.

Theory—the seeing of patterns, showing the forest as well as the trees—theory can be a dew that rises from the earth and collects in the rain cloud and returns to earth over and

---

3. Barbara Ehrenreich and Deirdre English, *Witches, Midwives and Nurses: A History of Women Healers* (Old Westbury, N.Y.: Feminist Press, 1973).

over. But if it doesn't smell of the earth, it isn't good for the earth.

I wrote a sentence just now and x'd it out. In it I said that women have always understood the struggle against free-floating abstraction even when they were intimidated by abstract ideas. I don't want to write that kind of sentence now, the sentence that begins "Women have always. . . ." We started by rejecting the sentences that began "Women have always had an instinct for mothering" or "Women have always and everywhere been in subjugation to men." If we have learned anything in these years of late twentieth-century feminism, it's that that "always" blots out what we really need to know: When, where, and under what conditions has the statement been true?

The absolute necessity to raise these questions in the world: where, when, and under what conditions have women acted and been acted on, as women? Wherever people are struggling against subjection, the specific subjection of women, through our location in a female body, from now on has to be addressed. The necessity to go on speaking of it, refusing to let the discussion go on as before, speaking where silence has been advised and enforced, not just about our subjection, but about our active presence and practice as women. We believed (I go on believing) that the liberation of women is a wedge driven into all other radical thought, can open out the structures of resistance, unbind the imagination, connect what's been dangerously disconnected. Let us pay attention now, we said, to women: let men and women make a conscious act of attention when women speak; let us insist on kinds of process which allow more women to speak; let us get back to earth—not as paradigm for "women," but as place of location.

Perhaps we need a moratorium on saying "the body." For it's also possible to abstract "the" body. When I write "the body," I see nothing in particular. To write "my body" plunges me into lived experience, particularity: I see scars, disfigurements, discolorations, damages, losses, as well as what pleases me. Bones well nourished from the placenta; the teeth of a middle-class person seen by the dentist twice a year from childhood. White skin, marked and scarred by three pregnancies, an elected sterilization, progressive arthritis, four joint operations, calcium deposits, no rapes, no abortions, long hours at a type-writer—my own, not in a typing pool—and so forth. To say "the body" lifts me away from what has given me a primary perspective. To say "my body" reduces the temptation to gran-diose assertions.

This body. White, female; or female, white. The first obvious, lifelong facts. But I was born in the white section of a hospital which separated Black and white women in labor and Black and white babies in the nursery, just as it separated Black and white bodies in its morgue. I was defined as white before I was defined as female.

The politics of location. Even to begin with my body I have to say that from the outset that body had more than one identity. When I was carried out of the hospital into the world, I was viewed and treated as female, but also viewed and treated as white—by both Black and white people. I was located by color and sex as surely as a Black child was located by color and sex—though the implications of white identity were mystified by the presumption that white people are the center of the universe.

To locate myself in my body means more than under-standing what it has meant to me to have a vulva and clit-oris and uterus and breasts. It means recognizing this white skin, the places it has taken me, the places it has not let me go.

The body I was born into was not only female and white, but Jewish—enough for geographic location to have played, in those years, a determining part. I was a *Mischling,* four years old when the Third Reich began. Had it been not Baltimore, but Prague or Lódz or Amsterdam, the ten-year-old letter writer might have had no address. Had I survived Prague, Amsterdam, or Lódz and the railway stations for which they were deportation points, I would be some body else. My center, perhaps, the Middle East or Latin America, my language itself another language. Or I might be in no body at all.

But I am a North American Jew, born and raised three thousand miles from the war in Europe.

Trying as women to see from the center. "A politics," I wrote once, "of asking women's questions."[4] We are not "the woman question" asked by somebody else; we are the women who ask the questions.

Trying to see so much, aware of so much to be seen, brought into the light, changed. Breaking down again and again the false male universal. Piling piece by piece of concrete experience side by side, comparing, beginning to discern patterns. Anger, frustration with Marxist or Leftist dismissals of these questions, this struggle. Easy now to call this disillusionment facile, but the anger was deep, the frustration real, both in personal relationships and political organizations. I wrote in 1975: *Much of what is narrowly termed "politics" seems to rest on a longing for certainty even at the cost of honesty, for an*

4. Adrienne Rich, *On Lies, Secrets, and Silence: Selected Prose 1966–1978* (New York: W. W. Norton, 1979), p. 17.

analysis which, once given, need not be reexamined. Such is the deadendedness—for women—of Marxism in our time. [5]

And it has felt like a dead end wherever politics has been externalized, cut off from the ongoing lives of women or of men, rarefied into an elite jargon, an enclave, defined by little sects who feed off each others' errors.

But even as we shrugged away Marx along with the academic Marxists and the sectarian Left, some of us, calling ourselves radical feminists, never meant anything less by women's liberation than the creation of a society without domination; we never meant less than the making new of all relationships. The problem was that we did not know whom we meant when we said "we."

The power men everywhere wield over women, power which has become a model for every other form of exploitation and illegitimate control. [6] I wrote these words in 1978 at the end of an essay called "Compulsory Heterosexuality and Lesbian Existence." Patriarchy as the "model" for other forms of domination—this idea was not original with me. It has been put forward insistently by white Western feminists, and in 1972 I had quoted from Lévi-Strauss: *I would go so far as to say that even before slavery or class domination existed, men built an approach to women that would serve one day to introduce differences among us all.* [7]

Living for fifty-some years, having watched even minor bits of history unfold, I am less quick than I once was to search for

5. *Ibid.*, p. 193.

[A.R., 1986: For a vigorous indictment of dead-ended Marxism and a call to "revolution in permanence," see Raya Dunayevskaya, *Women's Liberation and the Dialectics of Revolution* (Atlantic Highlands, N.J.: Humanities Press, 1985).]

6. Adrienne Rich, "Compulsory Heterosexuality and Lesbian Existence," this book, above, p. 68.

7. Rich, *On Lies, Secrets, and Silence,* p. 84.

single "causes" or origins in dealings among human beings. But suppose that we could trace back and establish that patriarchy has been everywhere the model. To what choices of action does that lead us in the present? Patriarchy exists nowhere in a pure state; we are the latest to set foot in a tangle of oppressions grown up and around each other for centuries. This isn't the old children's game where you choose one strand of color in the web and follow it back to find your prize, ignoring the others as mere distractions. The prize is life itself, and most women in the world must fight for their lives on many fronts at once.

We . . . often find it difficult to separate race from class from sex oppression because in our lives they are most often experienced simultaneously. We know that there is such a thing as racial-sexual oppression which is neither solely racial nor solely sexual. . . . We need to articulate the real class situation of persons who are not merely raceless, sexless workers but for whom racial and sexual oppression are significant determinants in their working/economic lives.

This is from the 1977 Combahee River Collective statement, a major document of the U.S. women's movement, which gives a clear and uncompromising Black-feminist naming to the experience of simultaneity of oppressions.[8]

Even in the struggle against free-floating abstraction, we have abstracted. Marxists and radical feminists have both done this. Why not admit it, get it said, so we can get on to the work

8. Barbara Smith, ed., *Home Girls: A Black Feminist Anthology* (New York: Kitchen Table/Women of Color Press, 1983), pp. 272–283. See also Audre Lorde, *Sister Outsider: Essays and Speeches* (Trumansburg, N.Y.: Crossing Press, 1984). See Hilda Bernstein, *For Their Triumphs and for Their Tears: Women in Apartheid South Africa* (London: International Defence and Aid Fund, 1978), for a description of simultaneity of African women's oppressions under apartheid. For a biographical and personal account, see Ellen Kuzwayo, *Call Me Woman* (San Francisco: Spinsters/ Aunt Lute, 1985).

to be done, back down to earth again? The faceless, sexless, raceless proletariat. The faceless, raceless, classless category of "all women." Both creations of white Western self-centeredness.

To come to terms with the circumscribing nature of (our) whiteness. [9] Marginalized though we have been as women, as white and Western makers of theory, we also marginalize others because our lived experience is thoughtlessly white, because even our "women's cultures" are rooted in some Western tradition. Recognizing our location, having to name the ground we're coming from, the conditions we have taken for granted—there is a confusion between our claims to the white and Western eye and the woman-seeing eye,[10] fear of losing the centrality of the one even as we claim the other.

How does the white Western feminist define theory? Is it something made only by white women and only by women acknowledged as writers? How does the white Western feminist define "an idea"? How do we actively work to build a white Western feminist consciousness that is not simply centered on itself, that resists white circumscribing?

It was in the writings but also the actions and speeches and sermons of Black United States citizens that I began to experience the meaning of my whiteness as a point of location for which I needed to take responsibility. It was in reading poems by contemporary Cuban women that I began to experience the

9. Gloria I. Joseph, "The Incompatible Ménage à Trois: Marxism, Feminism and Racism," in *Women and Revolution,* ed. Lydia Sargent (Boston: South End Press, 1981).

10. See Marilyn Frye, *The Politics of Reality* (Trumansburg, N.Y.: Crossing Press, 1983), p. 171.

meaning of North America as a location which had also shaped
my ways of seeing and my ideas of who and what was impor-
tant, a location for which I was also responsible. I traveled then
to Nicaragua, where, in a tiny impoverished country, in a
four-year-old society dedicated to eradicating poverty, under
the hills of the Nicaragua-Honduras border, I could physically
feel the weight of the United States of North America, its
military forces, its vast appropriations of money, its mass
media, at my back; I could feel what it means, dissident or not,
to be part of that raised boot of power, the cold shadow we cast
everywhere to the south.

I come from a country stuck fast for forty years in the deep-
freeze of history. Any United States citizen alive today has
been saturated with Cold War rhetoric, the horrors of commu-
nism, the betrayals of socialism, the warning that any collective
restructuring of society spells the end of personal freedom.
And, yes, there have been horrors and betrayals deserving open
opposition. But we are not invited to consider the butcheries
of Stalinism, the terrors of the Russian counterrevolution
alongside the butcheries of white supremacism and Manifest
Destiny. We are not urged to help create a more human society
here in response to the ones we are taught to hate and dread.
Discourse itself is frozen at this level. Tonight as I turned a
switch searching for "the news," that shinily animated silicone
mask was on television again, telling the citizens of my country
we are menaced by communism from El Salvador, that com-
munism—Soviet variety, obviously—is on the move in Central
America, that freedom is imperiled, that the suffering peasants
of Latin America must be stopped, just as Hitler had to be
stopped.

The discourse has never really changed; it is wearingly ab-
stract. (Lillian Smith, white anti-racist writer and activist,

spoke of the "deadly sameness" of abstraction.)[11] It allows no differences among places, times, cultures, conditions, movements. Words that should possess a depth and breadth of allusions—words like *socialism, communism, democracy, collectivism*—are stripped of their historical roots, the many faces of the struggles for social justice and independence reduced to an ambition to dominate the world.

Is there a connection between this state of mind—the Cold War mentality, the attribution of all our problems to an external enemy—and a form of feminism so focused on male evil and female victimization that it, too, allows for no differences among women, men, places, times, cultures, conditions, classes, movements? Living in the climate of an enormous either/or, we absorb some of it unless we actively take heed.

In the United States large numbers of people have been cut off from their own process and movement. We have been hearing for forty years that we are the guardians of freedom, while "behind the Iron Curtain" all is duplicity and manipulation, if not sheer terror. Yet the legacy of fear lingering after the witch hunts of the fifties hangs on like the aftersmell of a burning. The sense of obliquity, mystery, paranoia surrounding the American Communist party after the Khrushchev Report of 1956: the party lost 30,000 members within weeks, and few who remained were talking about it. To be a Jew, a homosexual, any kind of marginal person was to be liable for suspicion of being "Communist." A blanketing snow had begun to drift over the radical history of the United States.

And, though parts of the North American feminist movement actually sprang from the Black movements of the sixties

11. Lillian Smith, "Autobiography as a Dialogue between King and Corpse," in *The Winner Names the Age*, ed. Michelle Cliff (New York: W. W. Norton, 1978), p. 189.

and the student left, feminists have suffered not only from the burying and distortion of women's experience, but from the overall burying and distortion of the great movements for social change.[12]

The first American woman astronaut is interviewed by the liberal-feminist editor of a mass-circulation women's magazine. She is a splendid creature, healthy, young, thick dark head of hair, scientific degrees from an elite university, an athletic self-confidence. She is also white. She speaks of the future of space, the potential uses of space colonies by private industry, especially for producing materials which can be advantageously processed under conditions of weightlessness. Pharmaceuticals, for example. By extension one thinks of chemicals. Neither of these two spirited women speak of the alliances between the military and the "private" sector of the North American economy. Nor do they speak of Depo-Provera, Valium, Librium, napalm, dioxin. *When big companies decide that it's now to their advantage to put a lot of their money into production of materials in space . . . we'll really get the funding that we need,* says the astronaut. No mention of who "we" are and what "we" need funding for; no questions about the poisoning and impoverishment of women here on earth or of the earth itself. Women, too, may leave the earth behind.[13]

The astronaut is young, feels her own power, works hard for her exhilaration. She has swung out over the earth and come back, one more time passed all the tests. It's not that I expect her to come back to earth as Cassandra. But this experience of

12. See Elly Bulkin, "Hard Ground: Jewish Identity, Racism, and Anti-Semitism," in E. Bulkin, M. B. Pratt, and B. Smith, *Yours in Struggle: Three Feminist Perspectives on Anti-Semitism and Racism* (Brooklyn, N.Y.: Long Haul, 1984; distributed by Firebrand Books, 141 The Commons, Ithaca, NY 14850).

13. *Ms.* (January 1984): 86.

hers has nothing as yet to do with the liberation of women. A female proletariat—uneducated, ill nourished, unorganized, and largely from the Third World—will create the profits which will stimulate the "big companies" to invest in space.

On a split screen in my brain I see two versions of her story: the backward gaze through streaming weightlessness to the familiar globe, pale blue and green and white, the strict and sober presence of it, the true intuition of relativity battering the heart;

and the swiftly calculated move to a farther suburb, the male technocrats and the women they have picked and tested, leaving the familiar globe behind: the toxic rivers, the cancerous wells, the strangled valleys, the closed-down urban hospitals, the shattered schools, the atomic desert bloom-ing, the lilac suckers run wild, the blue grape hyacinths spreading, the ailanthus and kudzu doing their final desper-ate part—the beauty that won't travel, that can't be stolen away.

A movement for change lives in feelings, actions, and words. Whatever circumscribes or mutilates our feelings makes it more difficult to act, keeps our actions reactive, repetitive: abstract thinking, narrow tribal loyalties, every kind of self-righteousness, the arrogance of believing ourselves at the cen-ter. It's hard to look back on the limits of my understand-ing a year, five years ago—how did I look without seeing, hear without listening? It can be difficult to be generous to earlier selves, and keeping faith with the continuity of our journeys is especially hard in the United States, where iden-tities and loyalties have been shed and replaced without a tremor, all in the name of becoming "American." Yet how, except through ourselves, do we discover what moves other people to change? Our old fears and denials—what helps us let go of them? What makes us decide we have to re-educate ourselves, even those of us with "good" educations? A politicized life ought to sharpen both the senses and the memory.

The difficulty of saying I—a phrase from the East German novelist Christa Wolf.[14] But once having said it, as we realize the necessity to go further, isn't there a difficulty of saying "we"? *You cannot speak for me. I cannot speak for us.* Two thoughts: there is no liberation that only knows how to say "I"; there is no collective movement that speaks for each of us all the way through.

And so even ordinary pronouns become a political problem.[15]

- 64 cruise missiles in Greenham Common and Molesworth.
- 112 at Comiso.
- 96 Pershing II missiles in West Germany.
- 96 for Belgium and the Netherlands.

That is the projection for the next few years.[16]

- Thousands of women, in Europe and the United States, saying *no* to this and to the militarization of the world.

An approach which traces militarism back to patriarchy and patriarchy back to the fundamental quality of maleness can be demoralizing and even paralyzing. . . . Perhaps it is possible to be less fixed on the discovery of "original causes." It might be

14. Christa Wolf, *The Quest for Christa T*, trans. Christopher Middleton (New York: Farrar, Straus & Giroux, 1970), p. 174.
15. See Bernice Reagon, "Turning the Century," in Smith, pp. 356–368; Bulkin, pp. 103, 190–193.
16. Information as of May 1984, thanks to the War Resisters League.

more useful to ask, How do these values and behaviors get repeated generation after generation? [17]

The valorization of manliness and masculinity. The armed forces as the extreme embodiment of the patriarchal family. The archaic idea of women as a "home front" even as the missiles are deployed in the backyards of Wyoming and Mutlangen. The growing urgency that an anti-nuclear, anti-militarist movement must be a feminist movement, must be a socialist movement, must be an anti-racist, anti-imperialist movement. That it's not enough to fear for the people we know, our own kind, ourselves. Nor is it empowering to give ourselves up to abstract terrors of pure annihilation. The anti-nuclear, anti-military movement cannot sweep away the missiles as a movement to save white civilization in the West.

The movement for change is a changing movement, changing itself, demasculinizing itself, de-Westernizing itself, becoming a critical mass that is saying in so many different voices, languages, gestures, actions: *It must change; we ourselves can change it.*

We who are not the same. We who are many and do not want to be the same.

Trying to watch myself in the process of writing this, I keep coming back to something Sheila Rowbotham, the British socialist feminist, wrote in *Beyond the Fragments:*

> *A movement helps you to overcome some of the oppressive distancing of theory and this has been a . . . continuing creative endeavour of women's liberation. But some paths are not mapped and our footholds vanish. . . . I see what I'm writing as part of a wider*

17. Cynthia Enloe, *Does Khaki Become You? The Militarisation of Women's Lives* (London: Pluto Press, 1983), ch. 8.

*claiming which is beginning. I am part of the difficulty myself. The
difficulty is not out there.* [18]

My difficulties, too, are not out there—except in the social
conditions that make all this necessary. I do not any longer
believe—my feelings do not allow me to believe—that the
white eye sees from the center. Yet I often find myself thinking
as if I still believed that were true. Or, rather, my thinking
stands still. I feel in a state of arrest, as if my brain and heart
were refusing to speak to each other. My brain, a woman's
brain, has exulted in breaking the taboo against women think-
ing, has taken off on the wind, saying, *I am the woman who asks
the questions.* My heart has been learning in a much more
humble and laborious way, learning that feelings are useless
without facts, that all privilege is ignorant at the core.

The United States has never been a white country, though it
has long served what white men defined as their interests. The
Mediterranean was never white. England, northern Europe, if
ever absolutely white, are so no longer. In a Leftist bookstore
in Manchester, England, a Third World poster: *WE ARE
HERE BECAUSE YOU WERE THERE.* In Europe there
have always been the Jews, the original ghetto dwellers, iden-
tified as a racial type, suffering under pass laws and special entry
taxes, enforced relocations, massacres: the scapegoats, the
aliens, never seen as truly European but as part of that darker
world that must be controlled, eventually exterminated. Today
the cities of Europe have new scapegoats as well: the diaspora
from the old colonial empires. Is anti-Semitism the model for
racism, or racism for anti-Semitism? Once more, where does
the question lead us? Don't we have to start here, where we

18. Sheila Rowbotham, Lynne Segal, and Hilary Wainwright, *Beyond the Frag-
ments: Feminism and the Making of Socialism* (Boston: Alyson, 1981), pp. 55–56.

are, forty years after the Holocaust, in the churn of Middle
Eastern violence, in the midst of decisive ferment in South
Africa—not in some debate over origins and precedents, but
in the recognition of simultaneous oppressions?

I've been thinking a lot about the obsession with origins. It
seems a way of stopping time in its tracks. The sacred Neolithic
triangles, the Minoan vases with staring eyes and breasts, the
female figurines of Anatolia—weren't they concrete evidence
of a kind, like Sappho's fragments, for earlier woman-affirming
cultures, cultures that enjoyed centuries of peace? But haven't
they also served as arresting images, which kept us attached
and immobilized? Human activity didn't stop in Crete or Çatal
Hüyük. We can't build a society free from domination by
fixing our sights backward on some long-ago tribe or city.

The continuing spiritual power of an image lives in the
interplay between what it reminds us of—what it *brings to
mind*—and our own continuing actions in the present. When
the labrys becomes a badge for a cult of Minoan goddesses,
when the wearer of the labrys has ceased to ask herself what
she is doing on this earth, where her love of women is taking
her, the labrys, too, becomes abstraction—lifted away from the
heat and friction of human activity. The Jewish star on my
neck must serve me both for reminder and as a goad to continu-
ing and changing responsibility.

When I learn that in 1913, mass women's marches were held
in South Africa which caused the rescinding of entry permit
laws; that in 1956, 20,000 women assembled in Pretoria to
protest pass laws for women, that resistance to these laws was
carried out in remote country villages and punished by shoot-
ings, beatings, and burnings; that in 1959, 2,000 women
demonstrated in Durban against laws which provided beerhalls

for African men and criminalized women's traditional home brewing; that at one and the same time, African women have played a major role alongside men in resisting apartheid, I have to ask myself why it took me so long to learn these chapters of women's history, why the leadership and strategies of African women have been so unrecognized as theory in action by white Western feminist thought. (And in a book by two men, entitled *South African Politics* and published in 1982, there is one entry under "Women" [franchise] and no reference anywhere to women's political leadership and mass actions.)[19]

When I read that a major strand in the conflicts of the past decade in Lebanon has been political organizing by women of women, across class and tribal and religious lines, women working and teaching together within refugee camps and armed communities, and of the violent undermining of their efforts through the civil war and the Israeli invasion, I am forced to think.[20] Iman Khalife, the young teacher who tried to organize a silent peace march on the Christian-Moslem border of Beirut —a protest which was quelled by the threat of a massacre of the participants—Iman Khalife and women like her do not come out of nowhere. But we Western feminists, living under other kinds of conditions, are not encouraged to know this background.

And I turn to Etel Adnan's brief, extraordinary novel *Sitt Marie Rose,* about a middle-class Christian Lebanese

19. *Women under Apartheid* (London: International Defence and Aid Fund for Southern Africa in cooperation with the United Nations Centre Against Apartheid, 1981), pp. 87–99; Leonard Thompson and Andrew Prior, *South African Politics* (New Haven, Conn.: Yale University Press, 1982). An article in *Sechaba* (published by the African National Congress) refers to "the rich tradition of organization and mobilization by women" in the Black South African struggle ([October 1984]: p. 9).

20. Helen Wheatley, "Palestinian Women in Lebanon: Targets of Repression," *TWANAS, Third World Student Newspaper,* University of California, Santa Cruz (March 1984).

woman tortured for joining the Palestinian Resistance, and read:

> She was also subject to another great delusion believing that women are protected from repression, and that the leaders considered political fights to be strictly between males. In fact, with women's greater access to certain powers, they began to watch them more closely, and perhaps with even greater hostility. Every feminine act, even charitable and seemingly unpolitical ones, were regarded as a rebellion in this world where women had always played servile roles. Marie Rose inspired scorn and hate long before the fateful day of her arrest.[21]

Across the curve of the earth, there are women getting up before dawn, in the blackness before the point of light, in the twilight before sunrise; there are women rising earlier than men and children to break the ice, to start the stove, to put up the pap, the coffee, the rice, to iron the pants, to braid the hair, to pull the day's water up from the well, to boil water for tea, to wash the children for school, to pull the vegetables and start the walk to market, to run to catch the bus for the work that is paid. I don't know when most women sleep. In big cities at dawn women are traveling home after cleaning offices all night, or waxing the halls of hospitals, or sitting up with the old and sick and frightened at the hour when death is supposed to do its work.

In Peru: "Women invest hours in cleaning tiny stones and chaff out of beans, wheat and rice; they shell peas and clean fish and grind spices in small mortars. They buy bones or tripe at the market and cook cheap, nutritious soups. They repair clothes until they will not sustain another patch. They . . .

21. Etel Adnan, *Sitt Marie Rose*, trans. Georgina Kleege (Sausalito, Calif.: Post Apollo Press, 1982), p. 101.

search . . . out the cheapest school uniforms, payable in the greatest number of installments. They trade old magazines for plastic washbasins and buy second-hand toys and shoes. They walk long distances to find a spool of thread at a slightly lower price."[22]

This is the working day that has never changed, the unpaid female labor which means the survival of the poor.

In minimal light I see her, over and over, her inner clock pushing her out of bed with her heavy and maybe painful limbs, her breath breathing life into her stove, her house, her family, taking the last cold swatch of night on her body, meeting the sudden leap of the rising sun.

In my white North American world they have tried to tell me that this woman—politicized by intersecting forces—doesn't think and reflect on her life. That her ideas are not real ideas like those of Karl Marx and Simone de Beauvoir. That her calculations, her spiritual philosophy, her gifts for law and ethics, her daily emergency political decisions are merely instinctual or conditioned reactions. That only certain kinds of people can make theory; that the white-educated mind is capable of formulating everything; that white middle-class feminism can know for "all women"; that only when a white mind formulates is the formulation to be taken seriously.

In the United States, white-centered theory has not yet adequately engaged with the texts—written, printed, and widely available—which have been for a decade or more formulating the political theory of Black American feminism: the Combahee River Collective statement, the essays and speeches

---

22. Blanca Figueroa and Jeanine Anderson, "Women in Peru," *International Reports: Women and Society* (1981). See also Ximena Bunster and Elsa M. Chaney, *Sellers and Servants: Working Women in Lima, Peru* (New York: Praeger, 1985), and Madhu Kishwar and Ruth Vanita, *In Search of Answers: Indian Women's Voices from "Manushi"* (London: Zed, 1984), pp. 56–57.

of Gloria I. Joseph, Audre Lorde, Bernice Reagon, Michele Russell, Barbara Smith, June Jordan, to name a few of the most obvious. White feminists have read and taught from the anthology *This Bridge Called My Back: Writings by Radical Women of Color*, yet often have stopped at perceiving it simply as an angry attack on the white women's movement. So white feelings remain at the center. And, yes, I need to move outward from the base and center of my feelings, but with a corrective sense that my feelings are not *the* center of feminism.[23]

And if we read Audre Lorde or Gloria Joseph or Barbara Smith, do we understand that the intellectual roots of this feminist theory are not white liberalism or white Euro-American feminism, but the analyses of Afro-American experience articulated by Sojourner Truth, W. E. B. Du Bois, Ida B. Wells-Barnett, C. L. R. James, Malcolm X, Lorraine Hansberry, Fannie Lou Hamer, among others? That Black feminism cannot be marginalized and circumscribed as simply a response to white feminist racism or an augmentation of white feminism; that it is an organic development of the Black movements and philosophies of the past, their practice and their printed writings? (And that, increasingly, Black American feminism is actively in dialogue with other movements of women of color within and beyond the United States?)

To shrink from or dismiss that challenge can only isolate white feminism from the other great movements for self-determination and justice within and against which women define ourselves.

Once again: Who is *we?*

This is the end of these notes, but it is not an ending.

23. Gloria Anzaldúa and Cherríe Moraga, eds., *This Bridge Called My Back: Writings by Radical Women of Color* (Watertown, Mass.: Persephone, 1981; distributed by Kitchen Table/Women of Color Press, Albany, New York).

Index